THE
ART
OF
LETTING GO

The Freedom to Be Alive

Christmas 2024
For all you taught
me and offered

John

John G. Pisarcik

ISBN 979-8-89309-772-6 (Paperback)
ISBN 979-8-89309-771-9 (Digital)

Copyright © 2024 John G. Pisarcik
All rights reserved
First Edition

TXu 2-444-767

Covenant Books
11661 Hwy 707
Murrells Inlet, SC 29576
www.covenantbooks.com

For all those men and women, lay and religious, whom I have encountered along life's journey and who struggled with not living up to expectations, this is for you. Letting go is a painful, raw, reflective, and liberating process for each of us. Your grace-filled presence made it possible.

To gain the freedom we seek, we must work hard. We must work not only on the obvious things that distort reality and truth but also on those underlying causes we do not see clearly.

To be free is to let go! Sharing your life stories, the pain you have known and lived with, and your desire to move on lie at the heart of this work. Hopefully, others who read this book will start the journey of discovery and find the joy that letting go can bring.

Whether at the early stages of your life journey or near the end, we all must master the art of letting go to free ourselves of any baggage that hinders our entire development as we journey along until our final act of leaving this world.

Rev. Liam J. Hoare, sP, a man, priest, transformer, believer, showman extraordinaire, and dear friend, this book is dedicated.

CONTENTS

INTRODUCTION

Joan Lunden said, "Holding on to anger, resentment, and hurt only gives you tense muscles, a headache, and a sore jaw from clenching your teeth. Forgiveness gives you back the laughter and the lightness in your life."

The Art of Letting Go allows each of us to examine those things that consciously or unconsciously hold us back from being fully alive, psychologically strong, and spiritually healthy. Hopefully, each chapter will allow you to find areas that need to be looked at in your day-to-day dealings with others. Could they be at the root of your discontent? Or is it possible that we are the actual cause of our tension, unease, hurt, or resentment?

We cannot, of our own accord, change the past. What took place yesterday is now a historical fact. As individuals, we can learn from those past historical moments. We want to ensure they do not control our movements, thoughts, and feelings today.

Bernard Melzer stated, "When you forgive, you in no way change the past—but you sure do change the future." I hope that this work allows you to have a brighter future. A truth that acknowledges all you have known and experienced up to this point. A future that, despite what went before, we realize that we have the power to change the future for ourselves. In doing that, we also change the lives of those around us. Each person who grows and becomes freer allows others to experience that freedom and joy and seek it in their lives. We become a beacon of light. We should not tell someone else how to live or change but allow them to see how the darkness has left us and how brightness has taken its place.

1

Sweet Revenge

Lord Baron said, "Now hatred is by far the longest pleasure; men love in haste but they detest at leisure."

Revenge comes easily. Events that disgust us cause us to lash out against the perpetrator, whether a person, country, or ideology. The disgust we feel wells up until we call for justice or, in most cases, simple revenge. We want to hurt our object of hatred/revenge the way they hurt us. There is a sweetness in seeking revenge for wrongdoing. It is one of the most straightforward emotions to justify for ourselves.

It comes easily to be humiliated, hurt, and used to the extent that we all want to lash out at the perpetrator. At times, it consumes us. Whatever took place is never forgotten, never far from the front of our memory bank. It influences what we do and how we react to similar events, consciously or not.

We desire to bring as much pain as possible against the cause of our pain.

In time, we believe we are justified in doing whatever we must to inflict pain on the person, the country, the ideology, and those who believe in it. Hence, they know and experience the same hurt inflicted on us.

We train our military to attack, maim, or kill the enemy. We do not teach them to shoot a particular person, generally speaking, but rather those representing the cause of our pain. We brand whole groups under the blanket of the enemy. We kill to eliminate the root cause of the injustice inflicted upon us.

Throughout our history, the history of civilization, we find generation after generation of people hating and seeking revenge on others because of what they believe, where they live, or what some of their fellow men or women have done that outraged us. We even ask God to bring crushing defeat upon our enemy.

Do we not read in the Hebrew/Christian Scriptures the following:

"In these letters the king authorized the Jews in each and every city to group together and defend their lives, and to kill, destroy, wipe out, along with their wives and children, every armed group of any nation or province which should attack them and to seize their goods as spoil" (**Esther 8:11**).

In **Psalm 41**, King David writes,

> My enemies say the worst of me: "When will he die and his name perish?" When one comes to see me, he speaks without sincerity; his heart stores up malice; when he leaves, he gives voice to it outside. All my foes whisper together against me; against me they imagine the worst: "A malignant disease fills his frame"; and "Now that he lies ill, he will not rise again." Even my friend who had my trust and partook of my bread, has raised his heel against me. (**Psalm 41:6–10**)

In many cases today, we use the courts to do it for us. We seek revenge through legal action. We want to ensure that persons are prosecuted and imprisoned for what they did. The death penalty is not even good enough. Vengeance knows no bounds. It seeks out the most significant harm possible. All in the hope that we will find satisfaction and justification for our rage, our burning desire to get back at the cause of our hurt/exploitation.

Johannes Brahms tells us, "Those who enjoy their own emotionally bad health and who habitually fill their own minds with the rank poisons of suspicion, jealousy and hatred, as a rule take umbrage at those who refuse to do likewise, and they find a perverted relief in trying to denigrate them."

Even when they can see the one who hurt them is punished, it is never enough. We often try to find new ways to vilify their name and bring insult against them, and still, we are looking for satisfaction.

Misery seeks out misery, which allows us to believe that revenge is okay. The more individuals we find who think and feel like we do, the more we justify our stance. Sometimes, that can be construed as correct, if not healthy.

I think of what **Owen Jones** stated, "Few would deny the importance of tackling online hatred or child abused content. The internet, after all, has become a key weapon for those who disseminate and incite hatred and violence against minorities, and for those who lose a horrifying threat to children."

Queen Elizabeth I used to say to those who betrayed her trust, "God forgive you, but I never can." A feeling many harbor to this very day. There is a desire to strike back and make the one who hurt, manipulated, and changed our lives feel and know the pain we have lived with silently in most cases. It eats at us like cancer. As time passes, resentment and anger grow deeper, eating at our souls. We dream about it; we recall it like it was yesterday. It is horrendously always a part of us. And so it seems natural to seek sweet revenge of some sort. The real question at the heart of our pain is whether that revenge will genuinely give us satisfaction and allow us to move on and regain our lives.

James E. Faust said, "Most of us need time to work through pain and loss. We can find all manner of reasons for postponing forgiveness. One of these reasons is waiting for the wrongdoers to repent before we forgive them. Yet such a delay causes us to forfeit the peace and happiness that could be ours." Or more succinctly, "Forgiveness isn't about condoning what has happened to you or someone else's actions against you" (**Jennifer O'Neill**).

Lewis B. Smedes wrote, "Our history is an inevitable component of our being. One thing only can release us from the grip of our history. That one thing is forgiveness." Or as **John Lewis** tells us, "Not one of us can rest, be happy, be at home, be at peace with ourselves until we end hatred and division." And in reality, that is what we want. Namely, to finally be at peace and free of the constant recall of the past and embrace the future free of that hurt.

It is that underlying fear that eats at us. Too many sleepless nights have gone on with this endless fear that it could happen again to us. The suspicion that we were partially responsible for what happened. When the truth is that we were never responsible for what happened, we were victims, even if it seemed like we gave consent.

"Fear is the most debilitating emotion in the world, and it can keep you from ever truly knowing yourself and others—its adverse effects can no longer be overlooked or underestimated. Fear breeds hatred, and hatred has the power to destroy everything in its path" (**Kevyn Aucoin**).

It is not easy to allay those fears. There has yet to be a quick fix known to this author. What lies ahead of us is hard work. We can do work to alter our lives as the events that initially changed our lives. In short, **the freedom to live fully alive**.

Thomas Szasz writes, "The stupid neither forgive nor forget; the naïve forgive and forget; the wise forgive but do not forget."

Many of us believe that we have let go of the past until someone says something that triggers memories of that time. We can watch the evening news or a movie and suddenly find that we are filling up with tears, rage building up within us over what we thought we had left behind. We realize we never let go; we are still captives of another time and events. The realization hits home that we have not rid ourselves of the albatross around our neck or soul. That realization alone hurts.

Sue Monk Kidd stated, "I learned a long time ago that some people would rather die than forgive. It's a strange truth, but forgiveness is a painful and difficult process. It's not something that happens overnight. It's an evolution of the heart."

The process of letting go is done in increments. We slowly chip away at what inflicted such pain into our lives. We chip away at what happened, what was said, or what was not done to protect us. The beauty of a diamond is determined by its clarity and how many facets it has. Yet each facet was slowly, deliberately chipped away from the original diamond stone until the artist was satisfied it was ready to be polished and presented like a precious stone. We, who want to be freed from evil perpetrated against us, must do the same. We chip and chip until there is nothing left to chip. Only when we can see the full beauty of our soul with perfect clarity are we ready to show the world and ourselves what it has missed. Namely, the precious person we always were but are now clearly seen as such by ourselves and thus by others. If we cannot see that beauty within, it is virtually impossible to radiate it to others.

Mackenzie Phillips writes, "Forgiveness is not to give the other person peace. Forgiveness is for you. Take that opportunity." Or, as **Josh Billings** puts it, "There is no revenge so complete as forgiveness."

Somehow, we believe that we empower the perpetrator if we forgive. Forgiveness has little to do with the person or persons who brought about our pain. It does have everything to do with how we feel about ourselves, whether we see that we can be complete and happy again. Forgiveness allows us to trust once again and feel safe, and that is within our control.

"Never does the human soul appear so strong as when it forgoes revenge and dares to forgive an injury" (**Edward Hubble Chapin**).

Buddha instructs us, "Hatred does not cease by hatred, but only by love; this is the eternal rule."

The question remains: Is revenge ever sweet or productive? One could argue that it continues the cycle of violence. If, on the other hand, we want to be set free from the painful loss of trust that we experienced, there is little doubt that all it does is perpetuate the cycle of hatred, animosity, distance, and the dark night of the soul. The healing process occurs only when we confront and express our experience of loss. The absolute freedom we seek begins with our introspection, the work of letting go of those dark feelings that call for an eye for an eye. The journey to wholeness starts now, and much work remains for us in the weeks and months ahead. To allow light where up till now darkness has reigned has begun. Allowing that light to shine fully so that others see the change in us takes true forgiveness and reconciliation. We do all this for ourselves. The time spent, the effort to let go and forgive, is done that we are whole. We free ourselves of the shackles that were placed upon our inner spirit.

Historical facts do not change. Don't we all wish that they could if it were possible? That we were defrauded, embezzled from, accused unjustly, molested, psychologically abused, harassed—sexually or physically, none of that changes. Nor that we might have been tortured and bullied till we wanted to kill ourselves or live with the memory of those we killed during wartime, horrors we witnessed of people dying before us, and we could not save them. Each event changed our view of life, other people, or our abilities. Those are all things that happened.

What we can do to be free is name each event and confront each demon we face for what it is—an assault on our freedom to be fully alive. We set ourselves free as we let go of the power those events have had upon us over time. We learn to forgive, to see beyond that time to what still lies ahead. Otherwise, we continue to bring the darkness of the past into each new encounter we have or attempt to have with another person.

No matter how bruised, damaged, or torn apart we were, healing is possible through our effort to let go.

Michael J. Fox said, "One's dignity may be assaulted, vandalized, and cruelly mocked, but it can never be taken away unless it is surrendered."

And so you and I choose not to give in to what happened in our life, but we decide to move forward despite what happened. We refuse to surrender to the advantage takers, the bullies of this world. We become stronger each day that we make those deliberate choices. We determine how we are seen, what we believe in, and whom we trust. We are saying to those who so touched us in the past that you had your day; now it is my day. You had your moment when I was vulnerable, but now I am strong. Live with what you perpetrated, but I shall know that you shall not control my life now or ever again. Our growth, our ability to let the light shine through us and give hope and warmth to others, is our revenge. And that revenge is sweet. It shows the world that no one person or event can debilitate us, so we cannot overcome and do more than survive. We can be a source of strength for others who follow in our footsteps.

We are no longer the victims. Today, the choice is ours regarding how we wish to move forward. We can carry years of painful baggage wherever we go or deliberately choose to leave each piece of luggage behind us. You and I can set ourselves free. We shall never forget what took place, but we can forgive by releasing that pent-up anger within us. We can forgive and remind ourselves that was then, but this day is mine to do with what I like. I choose to free myself from events, words, and deeds that debilitated me and made me feel unloved, used, and uncared for by others.

This day is when I decide who I trust, who I reach out to, and whom I love. In doing that, I defeat the hold of the past. I release new energy and vision of what still can be for me and those around me. Hope is restored, love is allowed, and hatred is displaced.

Revenge is not sweet. It is bitter and fosters bitterness. Life is precious and allows us to blossom in a new day's sun. Choose life over revenge—light over darkness, life over hatred, and glory over bitterness. Grasp your self-worth and personal dignity and move toward that end over hatred and revenge. Accept that you were created out of goodness and choose to move toward that end. Let no one, not even yourself, tell you otherwise. Events in our daily lives do not determine our value; it lies in the fact that we are.

2

The Gem Within

This chapter reminds me of a man, an older adult by all counts, a priest of the Roman Catholic Church. We will call him Fr. James. A man who has manifested what being a gem is all about. He is a man not without his faults, but he has learned to deal with them while always reaching out and touching other humans to be all they were meant to be. Fr. Jim listens; he reaches out and offers a sense of healing that is rare and hard to find. Well into his eighties, he continues serving the Church and community. Fr. Jim is what I hope we are all like at the end of our journey. Someone who knows and understands who he is accepts who he is and celebrates life each day, lifting others to a better appreciation of themselves and their world.

Many of us struggle with self-image and how we see ourselves compared to those around us. How often did we hear parents or teachers say, "Why couldn't you be like your brother/sister?" It might arise because we were constantly compared to our siblings, who went before or after us.

We look at magazines, watch TV, and see ads for what we should wear; how we could look if we bought this product; or what type of body we should strive to achieve to be attractive to others.

After years of listening to what others say about us and seeing what advertisers believe we should look like in public, we wonder if we will ever be liked or accepted as we are. We begin to forget that, as individuals, we should be different from those around us, even our siblings.

Our differences make us who we are, and we are not molded into the image of someone we are not meant to be. Because we are individuals, we can see the world around us differently. We can see beauty where others see ugliness. It is what makes me and not you. Think of a puzzle box. The cover of the box portrays the finished product. The challenge is you and I are like that puzzle. Each of us is different from the others. Because of our unique differences, we add something no one else could bring. Maybe it is our shape, color, or how different puzzle pieces will never come together without us. We come into this world as priceless. Our life is needed. I do not need to compare myself to others because they have their unique place in this world as I do. If we all looked the same and were the same, it would be impossible to put the puzzle of life together.

A person comes across a stone. At first, it looks like any other stone—just a chunk of hard material like so many others lying around the ground. However, as we look closer and hold it up to the sky to allow the sunlight to cut through the dirt, we spot something different about this stone. There seems to be a glimmer of light reflected back at the sun. So we wash it in the stream and realize this rock might be of real value.

Upon having it checked out by a jeweler, we discover that it is a diamond in the rough. Its value will not be known until it is cut and polished to determine the stone's clarity and how many facets it will have. In reality, what seemed like ordinary rock is a priceless gem. The beauty lies in the finished product. Each of us is a priceless gem. As the years go by, that gem becomes more finely shaped; that which is superfluous is chipped away until we become a pure reflection of beauty. That is at our very core. It is who we are. Call it our soul, our center point, our true identity. No one can take that away from us or distort it. Only you and I are capable of doing that to ourselves.

Media, especially social media, can influence us so much that we lose a sense of who we are.

Instagram, TikTok, and Facebook bombard us daily with what others believe we should be doing today or how we should act or dress. Other people challenge us to do what they are doing or set a goal. At those moments, we have to ask ourselves, "Why?" Because we want to belong, to be part of the latest wave, we go about doing, and acting in ways we would never otherwise do, often getting hurt in the process.

Brigham Young asked, "Why should we worry about what others think of us, do we have more confidence in their opinions than we do our own?" Or as **Shannon L. Alder** put it, "One of the greatest regrets in life is being what others would want you to be, rather than being yourself."

We are that priceless gem. There is no other that can compare to our brilliance. But we have to choose to allow that light to shine forth. We have to become confident in the person we are. **Dan Coppersmith** wrote, "Our self-respect tracks our choices. Every time we act in harmony with our authentic selves and our heart, we earn our respect. It is that simple. Every choice matters." Do not allow others to make those choices for you. Please do not allow them to bully you into believing you do not fit in and are not important enough to be around them. It is those individuals who are not worthy of being in your presence. They are more concerned with tangible things than things of the heart or soul. They place value on being like someone else and not enough weight on the gift that they are. Many forms of social media have distorted reality for our children and teenagers. They watch and see others seemingly having a great time doing the day's challenge. They are encouraged to participate. Not to be left behind but to be part of the in-crowd. All done subtly so that the images and messages continuously run through their mind all day. The message is clear: If you engage in this, like us, you are cool, part of the "in" crowd. It does not matter whether the action is legal or dangerous; just do it and be like us.

Our ability to succeed in being someone in our own right has nothing to do with being part of the crowd. Many, knowing that they cannot do what they have seen or heard, simply drop into the background, feeling alienated, depressed, and not strong enough to be like those kids. And there lies the tragic error.

> "Don't rely on someone else for your happiness and self-worth. Only you can be responsible for that. If you can't love and respect yourself—no one else will be able to make that happen. Accept who you are—completely, the good and the bad—and make changes

as YOU see fit—not because you think someone else wants you to be different." (**Stacey Charter**)

Or as **Malcolm S. Forbes** has stated, "Too many people overvalue what they are not and undervalue what they are." We can never miss the opportunity to speak up, sound off, and be heard by others. Our voices, our views, and our values need to be heard. Whether they are accepted or appreciated is not of great importance. What is of great significance is that we have articulated something about who we are and what we bring to the group or community. Then our gem becomes recognized and may be seen for the first time. Sitting back and allowing others to make all the decisions that affect our lives is wrong. For too long, we have been encouraged to be silent. We accepted what those in authority said was right or wrong. We have been led to believe that they know better than we do what is good for us.

Churches, religious orders, and sects are notorious for telling their followers to live this way to be accepted and part of this communion. They are not God. Although the way they speak and write, you would believe they were. The Spirit of God works within every one of us. No religious body or organization has a monopoly on what is right and wrong. No government has absolute authority to determine how we have to live and what is lawfully right or wrong. Politicians, once in office, forget that they represent the people of their area. Their voice is incorrect when spoken to ensure the other side's voice does not prevail. Politics has become a dirty business and not a noble profession of public discourse. There is a need for change.

"Whatever course you decide upon, there is always someone to tell you that you are wrong. There are always difficulties arising which tempt you to believe that your critics are right. To map out a course of action and follow it to an end requires courage" (**Ralph Waldo Emerson**).

It takes great courage and self-discipline to be true to oneself. We want to know the core of our being and celebrate who we are compared to those around us. Sects, religious congregations/communities used to have, and some still do, all members dress alike. Religious garb did several things. It distinguished one community from another. It allowed the outside world to know that these men and women belonged to a particular community and followed the rule of their founder. Usually, the only distinguishing feature was the face of the individual; it reinforced the simplicity of life and the virtue of humility. Everyone was the same. Yet the reality was and is that they were not. Each man or woman who wore that habit was different. Each saw life differently. Years of training would try to break that individual, so they all acted similarly. They prayed the same prayers daily and sang the same songs/hymns together as one voice; they recreated for many in the same distinguishable habit. But the eyes and the facial expressions often gave you a glimpse of the real person. Some were cold as stone. Others had a devilish twinkle in their eyes. Some seemed to smile and laugh quickly while others always wore a constant frown or stoic look. Amish communities are easily recognized by the simplicity of clothing that men and women wear daily. As in religious communities, they are also governed by regulations and rules on living life. Most are made by elders, all being male.

For centuries, the Roman Catholic Church has controlled its members with endless regulations and laws. The Code of Canon Law makes one's head spin with its endless rules for all church members. Men make all these laws—in most cases, older men. Congregations of Women have always had to submit their way of life for approval to the Congregation of Religious. Again, a group of older men approve or disapprove of how these women see themselves fulfilling the vision and dreams of their particular foundress in their own day and age. As if these religious women were incapable of knowing what was best for the members of their respective houses worldwide. For all too long, we have held up the full development of people in the name of God. Because they were ordained, bishops were now more capable of understanding and empowered to determine what God wanted than those who serve God day in and day out in the field. Ordained prelates become a final voice regarding what we should or should not do to please God. They are not alone. Politicians and heads of corporations turn a deaf ear to the real needs of their constituents or workers. All seem to forget that without workers or followers, they are meaningless. Every organized body, religious or secular, has individuals who have risen to the top of the organizational chart. The position does not bring with it all knowledge, wisdom, and understanding. Every person who is in such a position must realize that without those who work under them their position is pointless. Without those individuals, they have no business, congregation, or real purpose within the community. Without compliance, congregations of women or men would not receive permission to live by the words they felt in their way of life to reflect their heritage and their calling. It was wrong in past centuries and is all so more today. It has been proven that Board of Directors does not get it right all the time and need to have membership changed in order to move forward as a company of corporation. Being alive demands the willingness to embrace change in ourselves and those we live with and interact with daily. Corporations, churches, and educational institutions must be at the forefront of change, not lagging. The disconnect becomes more apparent as workers are forced to strike to have their voices heard. Or as we see so often today, congregations of believers are separating themselves from their governing bodies because they no longer reflect the beliefs and needs of believers or those of the scriptures.

Our voices must be heard as knowledgeable people, and our ideas should be discussed frankly and openly. No one should be silenced because they call for a union or do not see the same way as those purporting to speak in the name of God or the board of directors. God has uniquely created each of us. We bear within our very being the image of the Creator. We can honestly know God's face only when we are all seen, heard, and bearing all our differences.

Instead, most of us, at the end of our journey will be welcomed home. We will be embraced and loved for who we are and who we became. We will be liberated from all the past constraints. We need not change for the sake of someone else who wants us to do that, for we were created in God's image. And God saw that what was created in us was good. It might take us a lifetime to see the same reality that we are good. We are priceless. We are a gem worthy of being respected and acknowledged in our own right.

Learn how to let go of all that says otherwise and let go of those who would drag you down—those who try to put you in your place. Your rightful place is that of a son or daughter of God. Your inherent dignity comes from the Creator. Our freedom comes from the Redeemer, and our growth to the fullness of glory from the Spirit.

The **Rev. Dr. Martin Luther King Jr.** said, "We are free, free at last." Let no person take that freedom away from you. Let your work speak for itself. Realize that no matter where we were born, no matter what economic background we came from, we are all called to become fully alive, genuinely aware of the suffering and needs of others. We can be beacons of light and hope in a world that would rather stamp out the light and crush our hopes and dreams. Or we can become docile, like sheep being led to slaughter. The choice will always be yours.

Suppress us, repress our steps, and we will still get up. Our resilience comes from within, not from the circumstances we find ourselves in. Our spirit already knows what we are capable of doing and becoming. You and I must not hinder that by insecurity, feelings of unworthiness, or of less value than the person next to us today. Stand tall, head up; you are where you are supposed to be. I do not care how often you have fallen or broken promises; today is your day to shine. Today is given to you as a gift, just as you were given to all of us as a gift. Value the gift you are. Be free to be. Amen! I repeat it. Amen to all you can be. Feel the warmth within you and know it is meant to be shared. Do not curse the day you were born but celebrate what today allows you to become. Each new day is a new challenge for us to grow and be more fulfilled.

Radiate the joy of being different from any other family member or community member. Today is not yesterday; that is already part of your history. Tomorrow has not dawned. But we have this day to blossom. We have this moment to be different and celebrate what lies ahead. And so we put one foot down in front of the other and begin our march. I do not need to be led or to follow. I need to accept who I am and have the ability and freedom to move forward. And so at times, I march with you; at other times, I take a different road. Constantly reminding myself that it is only one step more, one step at a time, that brings me where I am meant to be. Take that step, present the gem you are to others, and allow all those chips and scraps from the journey not to cloud your inner grace and strength. Those chips are not signs of defeat, bigotry, or bullying we may have encountered along the way but of our ability to brush them off, polish the person I am now, and say loud and clear, "Here I am, world, God, see me now.

I am not perfect yet, but I sure as heck am working on it."

We can then choose to belong to this community and embrace this way of life as free people. We do it not because it is what we must do but because, having been heard and respected as a gifted individual, we choose to live this way today. Together, we become a more potent force for good, complementing each other with our talents, wisdom, and love. It is a subtle difference but one that reflects that I am who I am, which is different from who you are. That difference brings mystery, intrigue, and surprises into each new day. A million words written are nothing compared to someone at peace with themselves. Let go of what you must to be that person. It is within your power.

3

Troubled Waters

The sound was thunderous as I sat at the cliff's edge at Mount Desert Island in Maine. Like many tourists, I witnessed and listened to the Atlantic Ocean as it battered the rocks below. The people of Maine call this Thunder Hole. The water rushes in an enclosed area, hitting the rock cliff with such force, especially today when a storm is brewing, sending sprays of water high into the air with a clap of thunder as the water encounters the solid rock. I marveled at the sights and sounds being presented before me. It is both magical and mystical. Nature at her furry, allowing us to see its power and awesomeness.

One clap of thunder made me jump back as I felt the water mist reach high up to my level. I clicked picture after picture, but those captured moments do not tell the real story of how frightening and wonderful that day was. People cannot hear the sound nor the ocean's fury as it beats against the cliffside, looking at a photo. They cannot experience getting wet from the salt water that rises above the cliff edge and sprays them in the face. You have to be there to appreciate what is taking place before you. On a calm day, this would all be missed. The spray would rise but never high enough to wet those standing and sitting on the rocky cliff. Oh, the waves would still crash, but without the thunderous roar we hear today.

During periods of our life, we may feel we have lost all control. That the forces of nature are working against us. We hear the booming voices of naysayers, those who would like us to disappear or never have been born. Some of us have been sprayed with the spit by our detractors. Or water cannons have been used to disperse us as we gathered to protest injustice to one of our own. Or because we breathe the same air as those who hate us do. But the truth is, we are equals. Others treat us less than humans, making us feel unworthy of standing on the same ground as they do. But we continue to stand and march until we are heard and fully recognized. We bleed as they do; we cry tears from the canisters of tear gas shot our way. Or the stones they throw, or batons that are smashed against our heads, our bodies. Yet we continue to get up, we continue to protest, and most importantly, we continue to be. Being free always comes at a cost. Our strength comes from deep within our being.

Our right to be present and heard lies in our birth. We all are born into a world that does not always welcome or accept those different from us, who speak differently or are sexually orientated differently. Our dignity does not rely on the color of our skin, the socioeconomic background, or the type of schools we were allowed to enter. Your worth and dignity lie in the fact that you are and have been placed in this world for a purpose. You are a unique creation.

Each day, it is essential, maybe even imperative, to take time for ourselves. We have to learn to be quiet. It is time to sit back and breathe deeply, exhaling the tension that hurts our neck, shoulders, and back muscles. We need to listen to our breathing until it slows down. When our heart is no longer racing or pounding in our ears. This quiet time is our time to recenter our life. We need to reenergize our battery to meet the demands made upon or expected of us. We must be at peace with ourselves in order to be at peace with others.

Women especially need this time. We have laid at their feet far too many expectations. Today, most women do not just care for their homes, husbands, and children. They also work as professionals. Still, they are expected to be equally involved in the community or workforce. We hold them accountable for dinner being on the table, laundry being done, chauffeuring, shopping, and listening to our complaints. And who listens to them? Who hears the lack of energy in their voices? We never realize how tired they are or how frustrated they are by all that is expected of them daily. They are not indentured servants within the household. They are women with needs, dreams, and desires they would love to see fulfilled. Do we even know what they are? Amid our complaints, how often do we ask them what they would like to see changed? What they need to feel fulfilled, appreciated, and accepted for who they are within this community, home, or family.

My mother found great solace just sitting at the beach and listening to the waves rushing in and out the shore edge. The rhythmic sound was both soothing and healing for her. It revitalized tired bones if you will. That time at the beach gave her a different perspective when she returned home. Or maybe it was the nights she just wanted to lay in a hot tub of water, candles burning, without someone knocking on the door or calling for her.

Howard Washington Thurman stated, "Don't ask yourself what the world needs; ask yourself what makes you come alive. And then go and do that. Because what the world needs is people who have come alive."

Or more graphically put, "It took many years of vomiting up all the filth I'd been taught about myself, and half-believed before I was able to walk on the earth as though I had a right to be here" (**James Baldwin**).

What has been said about us and what we have been made to feel about our self-image and worth can be changed. Each moment of the day presents us with that challenge. We can live in turbulent waters or calm ones. We can fight the current daily to stay alive or relax our bodies and ride the waves to shore.

Queen Latifah said, "I had to grow to love my body. I did not have a good self-image at first. Finally, it occurred to me, I'm either going to love me or hate me. And I chose to love myself. Then everything kind of sprung from there. Things that I thought weren't attractive became sexy. Confidence makes you sexy."

Perception is key. How we see ourselves affects how we see others and the world. The better we let go of preconceived notions about how we should present ourselves that are not true to our person, the healthier we will be.

The constant churning of our stomachs and the number of chewed antacid pills should tell us we are not at ease. Our number of headaches gives us a warning sign that we are fighting turbulent seas within ourselves. Yes, they may be influenced by those around us or our work environment, but it is our issue to be recognized for what it is. Many others go daily, walking the same halls we do and never experiencing the turbulence threatening to drown us.

Maybe **Louise L. Hay** was right on when she wrote, "You have been criticizing yourself for years, and it hasn't worked. Try approving of yourself and see what happens."

The sun will not always be bright and warm, which does not mean we will always have calm waters surrounding us. Days will still be cloudy, rainy, and limiting, but we will handle them differently.

Dr. Elizabeth Kubler-Ross wrote,

> The most beautiful people we have known are those who have known defeat, known suffering, known struggle, known loss and have found their way out of the depths. These persons have an appreciation, sensitivity, and an understanding of life that fills them with compassion, gentleness, and a deep, loving concern. Beautiful people do not just happen.

None of us want our children to experience the pain, struggles, and hardships we have had to endure. We try to shelter our offspring from having to go through them. But all too often, we are thrown into those situations no matter how hard we try. We can flap our arms wildly to keep our heads afloat, or we can lie on our back, arms out at our side, breathing deeply in and out, and float and go with the flow.

As a young man, I went to the country club to swim with my grandfather. I watched him and was mesmerized by his ease in the lake. You could always spot him from the shoreline. With the big belly and the black swimming trunks, he was the man floating in the water, hands behind his head and smoking his cigar. It was the rising smoke line from the cigar that gave his location. Gramp would smoke away and float effortlessly on the water for forty-five minutes. It was his way to relax, recharge his battery, and think through the issues confronting him. Not only was he a grandfather, but he was also a husband, father, volunteer firefighter, American Legion commander, and mayor of the largest township in the state.

He was never more rested than when he was floating on the lake or deep-sea fishing off the New Jersey coast. He loved the battle between man and fish. We used to catch a lot of Bluefish, and once, he caught a gigantic tuna. It took three additional men to help him bring it on board. He talked/bragged about it for months afterward.

The ocean can be peaceful, but it can also be dangerous in times of hurricanes. What makes an individual a good captain of a ship or fishing vessel is their ability to handle whatever the ocean throws at the boat. As ship captains, it takes all the skills they have acquired to ensure they are not broadsided by a wave capable of toppling the vessel.

We are the captains of our destiny. For most of our lives, we live with tranquil waters around us. But sometimes, we are called to rely on everything we have learned and observed over the years to keep our heads afloat. We battle waves strong enough to knock us off-kilter. They are capable of destroying us if we allow that to happen.

How many young men and women have found those turbulent times too great for them and taken their own lives? So many were harassed, bullied, and frightened even to go to school because they could no longer handle what was thrown at them. Some, who seemed so successful and full of talent and leadership abilities, could not take the responsibility and expectations put upon them. One day, they said no more and took their own life to be free.

Society often saw those who did that as cowards and sinners for taking their lives. But we were not walking in their shoes. We did not understand the pressure they were under. So often, the righteous who called them cowards never heard their discomfort, inner pain, or sense of total worthlessness in the face of such odds. Every life lost is a clear indictment of us who lived with them, worked with them, and recreated with them. Were we so blind, so deaf, not to see and hear their cries for someone to listen to their story, their inner pain, or feelings of failure? We saw that retrospectively but missed what was happening at the time because we were too busy and engaged. We had eyes to see but did not see; we had ears to hear, but their inner cry was lost on us.

Maya Angelou said, "You may encounter many defeats, but you must not be defeated. In fact, it may be necessary to encounter the defeats, so you can know who you are, what you can rise from, how you can still come out of it."

We need people around us who encourage such action—individuals who will stand with us in the best and worst times. We often find out who our friends really are in the worst of times. They are the women and the men who continue to be there, present to us, allowing us to know they still offer their friendship, care, and love. Not that they may agree with what brought us to this time in our history, nor should we expect them to do that, but despite everything, they still write, visit, call, and allow us to know we are not alone. They will enable us to accept being human. Not perfect, but human and all that entails.

Hugh Prather wrote, "Before, I thought I was actually fighting for my own self-worth; that is why I so desperately wanted people to like me. I thought their liking me was a comment on me, but it was a comment on them."

"Life is not easy for any of us. But what of that? We must have perseverance and above all confidence in ourselves" (**Marie Curie**).

It is essential in our daily lives to define what is worth holding on to and what we should let go of. New parents find the things they fought over with their firstborn or second hardly phase them by the time they have three or four children.

As a new teacher, I thought the knowledge I shared with the adolescents who sat before me was essential and worth learning. Boy was I wrong! What was important was the interaction between teacher and student. If they felt they were being heard and respected for what they believed, it was far more critical than what academic knowledge I had to share with them in the classroom.

I recall vividly going to an away wrestling match. The junior varsity wrestlers were on the mat, and I sat in the bleachers. The senior varsity team captain came over and sat beside me. At first, he said nothing; he just sat there watching as I was.

He and I had many honest disagreements about the work assignments I gave the seniors in my classes and what I expected of them. Finally, he looked me in the eyes and said, "You have no idea what is going on down there, do you? You do not understand the rules, how the ref scores, or why he seems to be telling a wrestler what he is doing wrong?" I looked at him and said he was correct; it was one of the most confusing sports I attended as a faculty member. He asked if I wanted him to explain it to me. I told this varsity captain I would appreciate it very much. And so for the next hour, he explained every move on the mat, and it made sense to me by the end of his explanation. I thanked him as he got up to prepare for his match and the rest of the varsity team.

Two weeks later, the seniors were due to turn in a significant paper covering half their grade for that trimester. The wrestling team captain was among the first to turn his into me. I just looked at him and asked why since he had made it clear he would not do it. He smiled at me and said, "Remember how I asked you if you wanted me to explain what was going on at the away wrestling match since you seemed to know nothing about our sport?" I told him that I did. He then informed me that night that he decided that if I was willing to listen to and learn from him, he might start seriously listening to me and understanding what I had to offer.

It was a turning moment for both of us. We both had to let go of our impression of the other. We both had to admit we did not know something and could learn from one another. In letting go, we forged a common bond. We actually became friends. Whenever he saw me at a sporting event, he would call out, "Fr. John, you sure you know what's going on today?" It became our joke, our bond, our time to be free of preconceived notions of one another. We need to tell one another that we still need to learn much, and you may be the one who teaches me today. Do not be afraid to open up and share your story with others. Allow yourself to hear the words pour forth from the depths of your being and know that you own the story; it does not own or control you.

Have you ever thought about what it is like to give birth? For months, a mother feels the fetus growing within her. She senses the child's movement when it kicks and seems at rest. Her moods, disposition, anxiety, and joy directly affect this growing child. We know drugs, alcohol, and smoking can harm the growing baby. However, for the most part, the womb is a safe place for this growing fetus. It can easily move around in the womb's fluid and listen to its mother's heartbeat. A bond begins to form between the two of them long before the day of its actual birth. And that is a day of both pain, extreme effort, and utter relief when it is all over.

Only a mother understands the pain and the anxiety associated with the contractions that proceed the birth. Each set seems more intense; it takes more of her strength to get through them and keep on pushing. Yet she does it. Like so many women before her, she endures the pain, which can go on for hours, hoping that she will bring forth the child she has now carried and nourished over these last nine months. When the child is freed from its mother's womb, the umbilical cord is cut, and the new human is laid in its mother's arms, there is that moment of amazement, relief, and joy.

The baby, who has known the security of the womb that day, finds everything seems wrong. It feels the pressure of those contractions. It knows that a movement that it has not experienced before is taking place. The serenity of the womb is being shattered. It has lived in the womb's darkness and now finds itself, with one giant push, being pushed out into a different atmosphere than it has known. It can be in the hospital's bright lights or the light of its new surroundings that first strike the child. There are new noises, its lifeline being cut from its mother, and now it must breathe and start functioning independently. Not until it is placed in its mother's arms does the child find anything that resembles what it has known. The newborn can hear that familiar sound of the heartbeat it has come to know. It will learn to suckle at the nipples of its mother for sustenance, strength, and the knowledge that it belongs. A day of unexplained pushing and thrusts until it is set free. The gentle movement of the womb's waters is replaced with diapers, blankets, and lots of noise. Welcome to your new world, my child. Make of it what you will. It is the moment that your personal journey begins.

In an unguarded moment, when she was three or four, I heard my niece tell me of that day. She recalled being pushed and thrust into the hands of a person outside of her mother's womb. It was said in the way a young child speaks. These simple words tell of an unforgettable experience that day. She leaned against me as she told me her story. Once she said it, she moved on. Back to the book, back to giggling, back to being herself. Months later, I asked her about that day, and she had no recollection. Either sharing with me what it was like or telling me about it. Yet studies have shown that young children can recall that day and will share if they feel safe, that it relates to what they are experiencing. Our brains store all events in our lives. Some are recalled much more frequently than others, yet every event happening is in the vault of our memory bank.

On the day of our birth, the waters of life were neither calm nor gentle for mother and child. Yet when the final push was over, the last flow of water complete, the first cry of new life was heard, a calmness descended, and an eternal bond formed between mother and child.

When I was a young principal of a secondary school, I used to give the graduating seniors two quarters. As they quizzically looked at them, I said, should you ever find yourself needing to talk to someone when you are in college, in the military, or out working, pick up the pay phone, call me collect using those coins. There were no cell phones in those days. Yes, pay phones existed on all campuses and elsewhere for people to use.

I remember one of our graduates who called more than once to say how he was doing and to hear a voice he knew would listen. But when he called that night, Park Rangers had just rescued and taken him to the hospital. He had left his family and had gone on a self-finding trip across the country. He worked many jobs, sending letters back telling me of his adventures. The night he called he had been caught in an avalanche. His tent had been covered with deep snow. He wrote his parents and siblings the last message, knowing he could not dig himself out. The park rangers knew he was camping since he had paid the entrance fee and told them where he wanted to go and what he wanted to see. They were the ones who organized a search team. It would take them a few days before one of the team's long poles would hit the tent, and the digging would begin. When they found him, he was lethargic, dehydrated, exhausted, curled up in his sleeping bag with the letter he had written tightly held in his hand. They brought him to the hospital, where he was hooked up to IV tubes to feed him and supply needed fluids to his body.

His first call was to me around 2:00 am. As I came out of my sleep and accepted the charges for the long-distance call, I realized who it was that was calling. I listened to his story of how darkness had engulfed him, and only the light of his flashlight allowed him to write his last letter. He wanted me to know that he was okay and asked if I would call his family and tell them he was and would be coming home. I recall suggesting he call, but he was not ready to do that. He and his dad had some real issues when he left. I promised him I would indeed call them. And so at around 3:00 a.m., I made the call. His dad answered, groggy as I had been, and I waited until he realized who was on the other end of the phone. I told him about his son's near-death experience, how the rangers found him, and that he was recovering in the hospital as we spoke. The only thing he said to me was "Why did he call you and not here? Don't answer that I know." At that point, he handed the phone to his wife, who listened intensely about her second-born son and what he had gone through. She was delighted to know that he was coming home and promised me that things would be different. She was true to her word. Her husband and son would reconcile with one another. Oh, maybe not as perfectly as she would have liked, but she was dealing with two stubborn Irish men she knew how to handle when push came to shove.

We all learn, some faster than others; if we do not let go of those things that stop us from growing together as a family, community, or nation, it is our own fault. We must let go of pride, the need to be correct, holier than thou, and knowing more than the other. We must learn, most importantly, to be just us with all our good and bad qualities. Knowing that the other has the same quirks helps. Our destiny is not to be the one who always wins but the person who has eyes to see what others see and ears to hear what words are spoken or not by others. Hopefully, we can embrace the present differences and build on what we can. Rocket science it is not, but it is just as challenging to implement in daily living. To live is to let go!

4

Negative Energy

Linus always walked around with a dark cloud over his head in the Snoopy cartoons and made-for-TV movies. This was how he perceived life and all that was happening around him. Yet he is not alone in that perception of life.

Individuals can look at a glass of liquid and see it as either half full or half empty. It is the same glass and amount of drink but perceived from different perspectives. How do you see the world around you? How do we walk through an average day? Are we pessimistic about what shall be? Or do we see this day as an opportunity? For many, it is easier to see the negative than the positive. Finding fault in others, whether it is our employer, colleagues, nation, or world, is much simpler than accepting our limitations and eccentricities.

It was **Tom Hiddleston** who said, "Haters never win. I just think that's true about life, because negative energy always costs in the end." Hate can absorb us. It can virtually dictate our every move or ability to think rationally and process information objectively. Hatred, by its nature, is insidious. It eats at us. It distorts reality and closes our eyes to what is good and worthy of praise and association. Moreover, it lays the groundwork for us to choose men and women who feed on our hate and, in many ways, fire it up. There will always be, as there have been over the centuries, those who thrive on hate.

Negativity seeks out and feeds on negative thoughts, philosophies, and actions that foster and give fodder for our feeling the way we do. Daily, we are challenged to see life and all those around us through the veil of hatred and disgust or through the light that distinguishes good from evil, individual persons from their actions, and people from policies. Even good people are capable of evil deeds. Much of our journey is finding out who is good from those who relish evil in all its forms.

"I realized that if my thoughts immediately affect my body, I should be careful about what I think. Now if I get angry, I ask myself why I feel that way. If I can find the source of my anger, I can turn that negative energy into something positive" (**Yoko Ono**).

Or as **DeMar DeRozan** wrote, "You gotta be able to take criticism if you want to be anything close to great. Even if it's not true, you use that as an advantage for yourself. You can use that negative energy and turn that into an energy that drives you to be something more than you thought you could be. That's one thing I did."

Bullying, name-calling, and damaging characterization of another are all displays of negative energy gone amuck. Unfortunately, in our day, we see many examples of this. Even politics and politicians have resorted to displays of inner hatred, maybe even rage, to incite others to action. Words have consequences. Negative comments or calls for destruction or individual harm have no place in a civilized society. What are we to do when we find ourselves in situations where it is evident that this person or group of people is here to feed on the negativity of the speaker? I can stay, or I can walk away. If we stay because we are too embarrassed to get up and go because we do not want to get absorbed by the negative energy around us, I am the real loser. This is one of those moments that call for heroic action, a bravery we did not know we had until that moment.

"I have walked away from friendships when I've realized that someone smiles to someone's face and talks about them the minute they walk out of a room. I have no room in my life for that kind of negative energy anymore" (**Sophia Bush**).

We have often been in situations that we instinctively knew were not right. There is no doubt that we can feel negative energy around us. Have you ever walked into a room filled with people and felt a cold chill run up and down your spine? Our body senses that something is amiss or outright wrong in this place, this setting. It warns us internally to be on our guard. Rather than walking out, we sit or mingle with some of the others—almost the feeling we have in watching a bad movie at the theater. After the first fifteen minutes, we know it is not going anywhere. The script is poorly written, and the actors are even worse at delivering their lines, yet there we sit. Are we too embarrassed to get up and make our way down the row of seats to the aisle and bother all those watching it? Probably! Or maybe we hope it cannot get any worse and improve as it goes on. It never improves and remains a movie I should never have paid to see.

Life is like that in many ways. Some days, we are captivated by what occurs in front and all around us—the small miracles of our day. Then there are those other days when we seriously question why we got out of bed in the morning. It would have been better if we had just stayed under the covers and not experienced the drama, the constant dilemmas we had to deal with during our waking hours. With or without us—life goes on. How we fit in and how we interact with others can and should make a difference. There is no person alive who is not worthy of recognition or does not have something of value to teach all of us. Most of the time, what is missing is our ability to listen. We are too busy to stop and hear what they have to say or maybe even look at them. We rush past, hoping they do not try to speak to us. Or, worse yet, we give superficial attention to what they tell us or who they are. A youngster or elderly adult, street beggar or corporate executive, saint, or public sinner, each one is put in front of us for a reason. Our dignity comes not from the position or lack thereof but from the core of our being. It is not their fault if I cannot learn from this individual. It is a result of my indifference, my feeling of superiority or entitlement, that separates us. Putting them down makes us the bully or the fool in the room. Wake up and look around. See what has always been before you but rarely perceived.

Bob Moawad penned, "The best day of your life is the one on which you decide your life is your own. No apologies or excuses. No one to lean on, rely on, or blame. The gift is yours—it is an amazing journey—and you alone are responsible for the quality of it. This is the day your life really begins."

Or to put it another way, "It's surprising how many persons go through life without ever recognizing that their feelings toward other people are largely determined by their feelings toward themselves, and if you're not comfortable within yourself, you can't be comfortable with others" (**Sidney J. Harris**).

I love this quote from **Victoria Moran**: "Did your mom ever tell you, 'If you can't say anything nice, don't say anything? She was right-and talking nicely also applies when you're talking to yourself, even inside your head."

Without realizing it, we spend energy every day trying to recognize our or others' expectations of us. Many individuals are overachievers. Men and women constantly push themselves to be better and more acceptable. That effort is a frustration we do not need. We are who we are. The person we are is a fine, okay, and lovable individual. Whether I feel that way or not, the reality does not change. God and your parents did not bring to life junk. They brought a woman or man into this world; they wanted their offspring to be happy and fulfilled in whatever they did.

Many of us firstborns realized early on that much was expected from us. If you were the first or only child they had, you quickly learned they expected much from you. You were a living reflection of them. Whether it was grades in school or extra-curricular sports/events, they wanted you to shine. Our brightness was and is an inner light, not necessarily manifested in all outward aspects of our daily living.

I never met my parents' expectations regarding grades in school. Like so many, I struggled with many subjects. Languages would always be a significant stumbling block for me—anything you had to memorize or learn through repeated use. I had tutors, went to summer school, and did what every kid who has "failed' in school knows all too well. All to no avail. To this day, I recall my homeroom teacher in high school telling me that college probably would not be the best choice for me. Yet being of Slovak, German, and Swedish background, I was stubborn and knew I would go.

College proved difficult, but I graduated with my A.B. degree in philosophy and science. I went on to graduate school and eventually received two master's degrees and my doctorate. I pushed myself to prove I was not as dumb as others thought I was or believed I was incapable of accomplishing. Yet I would continue to struggle with meeting my own expectations of what was expected of me. So, for much of my life, I continued to expend excessive energy trying to be the person I believed others thought or wished me to be. Instead of enjoying what I had accomplished, sharing with others what it is like trying to realize one's dreams can take its toll on the human psyche. I chose to keep pushing on, which would all catch up with me in time. Eventually, I would let down protective barriers and lose myself just to be accepted and loved for me. Not the degreed person or the ordained person I was supposed to be for others but rather the man before them. I was just wandering, searching for someone who reached out to just the man. I did it in harmful, illegal ways that would alter the lives of innocent individuals, families, and communities. There was no excuse for my behavior. I, like them, live with the consequences of my actions and betrayal all the time. Years of extensive therapy would allow me to understand the underlying causes of my actions. The hidden demons buried over the years finally broke free from the deep recesses of my psyche. Each of us is responsible for the words we speak and the actions or lack of that we engage in, no matter the reason. We cannot say "The devil made me do it" or any other excuse. We all exercise free will. And with it comes a tremendous responsibility to the truth, even if that truth hurts us in the process. It is an integral part of being free. It is essential if we want to grow and walk stronger than we were. Time does not heal, but it allows us to put in perspective all we experienced, learned, and changed to be the person we are today. And there lies our true strength.

We must do what is necessary to free ourselves from those demons. Otherwise, if not confronted, dealt with, and seen for what they are, we are doomed to repeat those same actions. It is, at times, when we have hit rock bottom, we are finally capable of letting go. Letting go of incorrect thought processes and misdirected emotions and needs. We must admit to ourselves the need to be healed to be an instrument of healing. We cannot be whole until we free ourselves of destructive behavior and thoughts. Let me assure you, it is not an easy journey that happens quickly. We worked hard at suppressing and hiding those faults within us. We thought we had them buried under control until we lost all control. They can no longer be buried or hidden; they are only seen for what they are and corrected as needed.

Even then, we have to choose. Do I do the work necessary to be whole, free, and accept my gifts and limitations, or do I go on believing I can handle this my way?

Doing it our way did not work out in the past; why should it in the future? Reaching out for help makes us vulnerable. We are forced to reveal and relive a life we have kept hidden. We have to hear ourselves admit we cannot do this alone. Trusting another individual or individuals with our history, the dark side of our life is never easy but liberating. We never knew whom to trust in the past with those parts of our life. Yet if we want to continue to grow and be the person we were meant to be from birth, we must let go of those fears. We have to embrace that this is not a one-person journey. No, others will carry us for part of it till we are strong enough to make the journey free of excessive baggage. Do I get rid of some baggage and keep some, or do I truly let go of everything that has laden me? Again, the choice is ours to make. The result is either freedom to live healthily or marginally.

The challenge is a fundamental one. We must accept our beauty and talents and celebrate them or concentrate on what limits, frightens, or holds us back. Yet if we choose to forgo that in-depth look at what makes us function like we do, we become our worst enemy. We deprive ourselves of the opportunity to become more than we are now. We stifle our own growth. We may hate those who suggest that we need help. Because we know there is nothing intrinsically wrong with us. But there is, and that is the point. One that I will not see for myself because it then calls for me to act upon it. It is far easier to blame others for not understanding us, encouraging us enough, or recognizing our exceptional abilities. It is not that others have not seen what we are capable of, but what we have become that calls them to act on our behalf.

There will be many dark and frightening days if we choose to enter therapy. It can be psychological therapy, psychiatric therapy, spiritual therapy, or a combination of them for us to become whole again. To see the world correctly and be part of the solution to what is needed rather than the stumbling block we have been.

Often, after a session(s), you will find your-self physically, emotionally, and psychologically exhausted. All you want to do is lie down and go to sleep. There is no more energy in the battery that keeps you going. We are like a piece of wet pasta. All we can do is cling to the wall, but standing alone is impossible. You will need your space, and those around you must accept that reality. At the same time, we must admit that we need our friends. We need sounding boards to bounce off our words, thoughts, and confusion that seek clarity. They might not be able to add any profound insight, but the mere fact that they sit there with us and listen should be sufficient. It is their presence that becomes life supporting. Some of the individuals in the room with whom I bounced hidden secrets off, I had only known briefly. Yet I felt safe with them; they lis-tened, held me when I cried, made me laugh at other times, and allowed me to see my own folly without judgment or advice. They allowed me the moment of their time just to be there. And that was all I needed to get through the following hours, that night, and the day to follow. Yes, I contemplated ending my existence because the pain was too great. I did not feel I had the strength or will to take the next steps. But these individuals helped put "Humpty Dumpty" back together with their concern, care, and quiet presence. Till my last breath on this Earth, I will always be grateful. They did not tell me that every dark cloud has a silver lining. Or the sun will come out tomorrow. Or that all pain eventually goes away. They gave me no false hopes or illusions. What they offered me was themselves, their physical presence, their human touch, and the knowledge that this was indeed an ugly time. In reality, that was the unspoken assurance that I needed right then. They took all that negative energy of mine and allowed it to dissipate in front of me. Because they knew how stubborn I could be, they allowed me to rant and cry out with all the force inside me. These individuals allowed it to all come out without trying to interrupt or change topics. As those words poured out of me, I could see them more clearly, less freighting or having a hold over me. These good men never looked at their watches or indicated that I bored them or was taking up valuable time—they just gave me what I needed right then and there. Now, that is grace in action. Saving grace is what I would call it. I know it saved my life. Every man or woman who has been addicted knows of what I write and speak. There is such a reality as saving grace. A grace that lifts us and allows us to move and live again. To put a dance back into our step, maybe even a smile on our battered lined faces.

Chamillionaire said,

> "I mean, honestly, anybody can diss me. I remember 50 Cent said something and everybody was like you need to get at 50 and I was like. "Whatever, I'm in a whole different place in my life." It's gon' have to take something really, really serious for me to start putting that much negative energy into the world again."

We can be free and not boxed in by what others say or think about us. For one, we have absolutely no control over their negative thoughts or feelings toward us. That is their right to believe what they want to think. We could try to convince them otherwise, but it is a waste of time and an exercise in futility. They have already decided about the type of person they believe we are. That is their issue; it is not your issue. Your life is what matters; how you go about living matters today. You control that; we must exercise that for our growth and sanity.

Sienna Miller reflected on that feeling by saying, "It's wonderful to feel supported, but there's a lot of negative energy towards me as well. So I ignore it, to be honest. If I started to read it all it would completely mess up my head."

Due to social media today, many individuals cannot avoid everything said about them. Nor is it easy to put everything you read or people say about you behind you. What we must do is know who we are today. Yes, what you said in the past may come back to haunt you, but it is in the past. Likewise, what you are scolded for doing in the past cannot be changed. What changes or does not change is your understanding of yourself and how you conduct yourself today. There lies your constant need to grow. All growth depends on change. We look around us and see what is occurring in nature all the time. Plants change before our eyes all the time. Without constant development or growth, they do not produce fruit or flowers. You and I patiently wait for that process to take place so we can enjoy what it produces. And so we must be gentle with ourselves. We need to recognize and accept the need for change. In doing that, we can let go of those negative things or demons lurking beneath the skin and transform ourselves into better, more holistic people. We reach our potential in constantly changing steps.

"Take the attitude of a student, never be too big to ask questions, never know too much to learn something new" (**Og Mandino**).

I recall reading, the author has slipped my mind, but what was put to paper did not. "You cannot control what happens to you, but you can control your attitude toward what happens to you, and in that, you will be mastering change rather than allowing it to master you."

A friend of mine, a woman religious, is the personification of the above statement. For many years, eight to be exact, she led her region as their Provincial. But those she served had other ideas. They choose her to continue to lead them for another four years. She was opposed and told them so. Their General Superior did the same. But her fellow sisters elected her again despite the calls to allow her time out of a leadership role. And so she entered her third four-year term.

Six years after her third term as provincial, she was elected by the entire Congregation to serve as the worldwide Assistant Superior General. Three and a half years into her term, the Superior General died, and she had to take on the duties of the Superior General. It was not a position she wanted, yet now she had to assume. Not only did she take on the responsibilities of such a leadership role for the remaining half year of their elected term, but at the end of that term, the women religious elected her to take on the role again for another ten years as their Superior General. It was not easy to accept for her, yet each day, she got up and was for them what they expected and wanted. Personally, those additional ten years in the highest position of leadership and authority would physically, psychologically, and spiritually take a toll. All she wanted to do was step out of leadership positions and live the life of a religious she had committed herself to many years ago and renewed every year since.

When I see pictures of her Congregation now that she is semi-retired and members gather from around the world for meetings, I see how happy they are to see her again. Their warm embraces of her and the smiles on the faces of the Sisters as they greet her tell us much about her years of leadership. She touched lives and led by example. She would be the first to tell you that mistakes were made during her time in office, but she did what she believed she had to do. I will always be grateful for how she personally continued a friendship with me when others had had enough, made their judgment, and walked away. She did not have to keep in contact nor share life with me as she has. She did not allow negative energy to consume or stop her from working. She rose above it, took on new tasks, and kept transforming herself to meet the actual needs articulated by those she once led. A woman of grace and a religious sister worthy of her calling.

Kahlil Gibran, in his works, writes, "Your living is determined not so much by what life brings to you as by the attitude you bring to life; not so much by what happens to you as by the way your mind looks at what happens."

We can transform what was negative into something positive. It demands work but is attainable. Good health of mind and body demands work. Spiritual wholeness requires constant work. No matter what we have gone through or what others have thought about or spoken about us, we change what we can still do and become. It is only when we stop progressing and changing that life becomes stagnant. That which stagnates is what stinks.

I believe we were brought into this world to celebrate life. Accept the ups and downs, the good and evil, and with the same grace, we receive good happenings in our lives. Tears and laughter make us whole. One releases the pain and the sorrow within, and the other acknowledges that everything is not severe or disastrous. Some things are light, easy to understand, and make you happy. Embrace both with the same dignity. If God does not create junk to be easily dismissed or thrown on the side, it is our task to allow all to see who we are becoming. Not who we have been but who we are today. What we will look or sound like a year or even a month from now is still to be determined. We are the captains of this vessel I call me. We can sail it into the safety of the port by embracing the individual at the helm, not with arrogance, but with the solemnity of God's grace working through us and in us right now. Let me end this chapter with a work familiar to many of you. Written on January 1, 1910.

IF

If you can keep your head when all about you are
    losing theirs
And blaming it on you;
If you can trust yourself when all men doubt you,
But make allowance for their doubting too;
If you can wait and not be tired by waiting,
Or, being hated, don't give way to hating,
And yet don't look too good, nor talk too wise;
If you can dream—and not make dreams your
    master;
If you can think—and not make your thoughts your
    aim;
If you can meet with triumph and disaster
And treat those two imposters just the same;
If you can bear to hear the truth you've spoken

Twisted by knaves to make a trap for fools,
Or watch the things you gave your life to broken,
And stop and build 'em-up with worn-out tools;
If you can make one heap of all your winnings
And risk it on one turn of pitch-and-toss,
And lose, and start again at your beginnings
And never breathe a word about your loss;
If you can force your heart and nerve and sinew
To serve your turn long after they are gone,
And so hold on when there is nothing in you
Except the Will which says to them: "Hold on";
If you can talk with crowds and keep your virtue,
Or walk with kings—not lose the common touch,
If neither foes nor loving friends can hurt you;
If all men count with you, but none too much;
If you can fill the unforgiving minute
With sixty seconds' worth of distance run—
Yours is the Earth and everything that's in it,
And—which is more—you'll be a Man, my son!
(Rudyard Kipling)

5

The Past That Is Always Present

Most live their lives getting out of bed in the morning and starting a new day. But for so many individuals, a new day carries the baggage of days past that refuses to let go. Moreover, that baggage can debilitate us from doing productive work today.

People around us think everything is fine with us. Only the individual knows that everything is not okay. Ask any man or woman who has been in combat and has taken the life of another. Ask someone who has destroyed another person's life physically or psychologically if today will be fine. The memories and horror they experienced always lurk deep within them. What will trigger those memories, and what sound will bring all the freight back again? Only they can anticipate, with anxiety, that they might experience it again.

I grew up with the generation before me who had fought in World War II. They were good men, solid citizens, who carried a burden that few of us even knew they carried. They never talked about what they did or experienced while fighting. At least, not at home, not with their immediate family. The wives knew but did not know. They knew their husbands had terrible nightmares that woke them from a deep sleep, dripping with sweat. Yet even then, their husbands just said it was a bad dream and did not want to discuss it; they just wanted to go back to sleep.

Back then, we did not know about post-traumatic stress disorder. We did know that many, when going to the American Legion and Veterans of Foreign Wars Hall, these warriors often drank too much and came home drunk as a skunk. There, with fellow war buddies, some of their stories were shared or told. Never all their personal stories, especially those that tormented them the most. But here, with these men, they felt a camaraderie, a safe place to let go. They knew the listener, probably equally drunk, had been there, done what they had, and had no one to listen to their pain.

Some carried visible signs of war. Lost limbs, sight, or hearing, and others had psychological scars that did not show. Life-changing events had taken place before their very eyes. They may have been the cause as they fulfilled their sworn duty to defend their country. Their country had called for them to battle, and they responded positively. Young men in their late teens and early twenties did as they were trained and told to do. They were shot at, artillery went off near them, and they watched fellow warriors maimed or die in their arms. There was rarely any time for tears because the shelling did not stop; the war continued. And they continued to do their duty for the country they honorably served.

A friend of mine, now deceased, went into the air force when he was eighteen years of age. Their plane was in many an air battle. He was in the tail gunner position. He recalls bullets coming through the sides of the aircraft in the heat of battle, wondering at nineteen and twenty if he would ever get home to New Jersey again. He would return but never be the man his wife fell in love with. He was different, withdrawn, silent, and ready to snap at the least frustrating thing. He would not talk about it with her or anyone else. He and his wife would have three sons they would raise and watch grow into manhood. He never encouraged them to join the armed services. Fortunately, they were not living with the draft or their country's call to fight a new enemy.

When the movie *Band of Brothers* came out, the three sons took their dad and mom to see it. They thought that because their dad had been in those fighting planes and battles they ultimately won, it would be a movie he would like to see. How wrong they were. My friend never made it through the film. During one scene of an air battle, he began crying in the movie theater, physically shaking and left his seat. They all followed him out and into the car. He cried all the way home as his wife held him as tightly as she could. She would come and see me the next day and tell me what happened, and if I could come to the house and talk to him, maybe he would come to work again. An employee he was, but he and his wife were also dear friends. They often referred to me as their fourth son. I assured her that afternoon I would stop at the house.

Before I entered the house, I knew I would not be going there to talk to him. No, I just wanted him not to be alone, to see me sitting beside him. And so when I arrived, his wife took me to a small room in the house off from the living room. There he sat, just staring into space. Present in one place, living in another. At first, he knew someone had entered. Someone who was like a son but more than a son. He looked at me but did not see me. He was some-where else. So I sat in the chair next to his. We both just sat and stared into the unknown. I did not know what was going on in his mind, what terrors he was reexperiencing all over again. I knew this man who worked for me, someone I had grown close to, was hurting badly. At one point, he turned toward me, tears running down his face.

He told me how he had to walk out of the movie theater. The film was too realistic for him. It was like he was again in the tail gunners' position. As the tears ran down his face, he reiterated that he was only a kid. Not even twenty years old, and here he was trying to take another plane out of the sky, as they were trying to do to their aircraft. He did not want to relive that; he did not want to recall or talk about those moments of terror. I assured him it would be okay if he did not discuss them with me today. All I wanted him to understand as I hugged this sixty-plus-year-old man was that he was cared for, loved, and needed at this moment: a wife who loved him dearly and three sons and grandchildren who also adored him. I assured him that his family would not force him to talk about it, especially since his sons did not think he was less of a man for losing it in the theater or on the way home. Instead, they wanted him to know how proud they were of him. They never learned what he did in the war or the extent to which the war was still very much part of his life, even today. A portion of his life that, like so many of his generation, did not speak about with their families.

We have since sent men and women to other places where they have encountered hostilities.

Today, we have them serving in countries where they are hated, yet they continue to do the job they have been trained to do. Whether or not each of them agrees with the politics that brought them to these places, they have sworn an oath to defend the Constitution and bear arms against all who threaten our democracy.

The Commander-in-Chief can change every four or eight years, the policies they enact these men and women enforce across the globe. We can never repay them for the service they render. Nor must we believe we know what they have experienced or buried deep within their psyche. They take up arms in all our names out of love for their country and family. We sleep safely at night because somewhere in the world this day, they stand guard, always alert to the danger around them and those who serve with them. We call them heroes, but they are just simple men and women doing a tough job. For many, the twenty-pound pack on their back is nothing compared to the weight they carry on their shoulders, heads, and hearts. The pack you can easily take off; the rest is not so easy. Letting go of the rest can be a long process.

Trauma, living with anxiety or fear for prolonged periods, takes its toll on any of us. Certain sounds never leave us. Many never want to be in the dark for fear of what it brings. Some form of light must always be on to dispel the darkness that can engulf a person.

Dr. Elisabeth Kubler-Ross wrote, "People are like stained-glass windows. They sparkle and shine when the sun is out, but when darkness sets in, their true beauty is revealed only if there is light from within."

Our ability to rise above the gloom, the darkness that can surround us all at times, lies not outside somewhere; no, it lies within our God-given dignity. Moreover, for those who hold there is no god, just life and death, again look deep within yourself for the strength to see and experience a new day. One that you determine how it will unfold. A day of infamy or a day of glory. As previously written, we are the captains of this vessel we call ourselves. If the "I" in me cowers under the covers for fear of facing the new twenty-four hours, there is no one to blame but us.

Jack Butcher stated it better than this writer: "You are not what you've done. You are what you keep doing." So throw off those covers, stretch those limbs, climb out of bed, and begin this day. It is to be your day, one filled with new possibilities, new adventures, and the opportunity for wholeness of body and spirit.

Whether you are a teenager, a young adult, middle-aged, or elderly, you must make the essential choice as to the direction of this day. I can leave my room already weighed down, or I can go with a smile on my face. It is better to put on that happy face and make others wonder what you know that makes you so glad that they do not understand. What you do know is that your happiness lies within.

In the **Dhammapada**, we find, "As a mountain of rock is unshaken by wind, so also, the wise are unperturbed by blame or by praise." Fear not what others say or feel about you. What must always be your concern is what you feel about yourself. Our confidence comes from that insight. Our ability to listen to what others say with empathy and understanding comes from our belief that we are worthy of their confidence, trust, and pain. And yes, it can be the opposite. Who knows what others say about them behind their backs that can ruin this day? But why allow it to do that? No, walk down the corridor, the hallway, with that smiling face of yours, maybe even with a bounce in your step, that makes them stop or sit up at their desk and remark, "What's with him/her like they don't have a care in the world? What do they know that we have not been told yet?"

"Bad things do happen; how I respond to them defines my character and the quality of my life. I can choose to sit in perpetual sadness, immobilized by the gravity of my loss, or I can choose to rise from the pain and treasure the most precious gift I have-life itself" (**Walter Anderson**).

The weather is stormy here today. Thunder, lightning, and torrential rain are coming down. It batters the windowpanes in the study. I keep hitting save to ensure that nothing written today is lost if there is a sudden loss of power. The generator takes about three seconds to take over, but those three seconds could mean a whole morning's worth of work lost or preserved. The sound of the storm is exhilarating for me. For others, I realize it can be frightening and a real downer to be caught up in such a storm. It is always a matter of perspective. And so I keep typing away, rearranging words, sentences, and my thoughts as I try to keep up the same tempo as the storm outside my windows.

Life is filled with moments like today. We knew this storm was coming from the weather reports. Yet can any weather forecaster convey how it will affect you personally? All they can do is give us the knowledge that a significant event will occur. How we prepare and cope with that event is your choice.

I recall vividly that we had prepared ourselves after we were told of a major snowstorm coming toward the United States East Coast. My neighbors and I were not ready for the amount of snow drifts that occurred. We knew where the snow shovels were and the ice melter we could scatter around after the shoveling was over.

In the morning, I looked out the window and saw that the roads and the cars outside were also covered. I bundled up, went into the garage, grabbed my shovel, and hit the garage door button to raise the door. What I saw took my breath away. I gazed out my open garage door at a solid wall of snow. No light came through, just a massive mound of snow greeted my eyes. The snow shovel in my hands looked worthless to me. I proceeded to go back into the warmth of the house. It would take two days for the city to plow through our neighborhood. Fortunately, the man who cut our grass over the summer also had a snowplow. He came on the third day and, with the plow, cleared the driveway. What a relief to know that if we had to get out, we now had a way to do that.

The snowstorm brought back memories of childhood. Snowmen were created, snowball fights ensured, sledding took place, and fresh snow was eaten. The incredible excitement was when my mother would announce that the radio said schools were closed and we had a snow day. For that moment, the past and present merged.

In our lifespan, there are many moments like that for most individuals. It is a déjà vu moment that makes us wonder if this moment is real or if our memory is playing tricks on us. Am I experiencing this for the first time, or am I recalling an event that happened long ago in my life? Our memory keeps locked up, for the most part, all our life experiences. Nothing that has taken place is ever forgotten. It's just safely stored away. Older adults will tell you, and I am now part of that group, that past things are very vivid to them. What we did this morning and yesterday seems to escape them. Yet they can recall events of long ago and conversations and things they saw and did as if they had just occurred.

The good and the bad are all stored away. Some, when they are recalled, bring smiles to our faces. Others bring a chill down the spine. All memories are not good ones. However, they are part of who we are today. We must learn to deal with or cope with those memories when they come to the forefront.

I read this particular quote on **Tumbler** in the section of "Personal Quotes," which I think is appropriate: "There are two ways to spread happiness; either be the light who shines it or be the mirror who reflects it."

Our daily challenge is allowing all we have become to this point in our lives to shine forth, to be a source of amazement or wonderment to those around us. To every adolescent or adult who is being bullied, please do not allow them to diminish your worth, your value, or what you bring that no one else can. Yes, we each bring something others do not have. That is our perspective on life and what is happening here and now. Each of us perceives events in our own unique way. No one in our group can see what we see. Police often tell us, when questioning individuals about an event that took place, that seven people can have seven different versions of the accident, the altercation, or the tragedy being investigated. All were present, yet each remembers it from a different perspective. Law enforcement's responsibility is to put those versions next to one another. Determine what is common in all and what might be a lead in what is not common in telling the event.

"Only I can change my life. No one can do it for me." Comedian **Carol Burnett**, in that simple statement, gets right to the point of this section. Regardless of the circumstances we find ourselves in or the conditions we are asked to deal with daily, we must look inside to see if there will be a real difference.

Earl Nightingale wrote, "Learn to enjoy every minute of your life. Be happy now. Don't wait for something outside of yourself to make you happy in the future. Think how really precious is the time you have to spend, whether it's at work or with your family. Every minute should be enjoyed and savored."

The past is the past. History records it and will make its own judgment regarding that time. I cannot change what was, but I can change what is and should be. That is always within my power.

Kevyn Aucoin states, "Today I choose life. Every morning when I wake up I can choose joy, happiness, negativity, pain... To feel the freedom that comes from being able to continue to make mistakes and choices—today, I choose to feel life, not to deny my humanity but embrace it."

Why curse the day you were born? Why blame others for mistakes or the pain you have caused? Embrace all your life. This author knows the joy of beautiful moments and has experienced the thrill of living life to the fullest. I have also known the darkest of times when my words and deeds changed the life of another for the worse. Those moments must be embraced the same way the moments of jubilation are welcomed, or we have learned nothing about ourselves and life.

If I could rewrite my history, I would do things differently retrospectively. That luxury is not ours to have. What we do have is the ability to grow. We take upon ourselves the task of facing both the good times and the bad and reflecting on them to see the underlying cause of what took place. Only then can we repair the harm done or build on what brought joy and fulfillment to others. Never forget to accept the whole package of who you are right now. We can lock ourselves in moments of the past and not be able to move from them. We can continue to repeat those same patterns or actions or say to our inner self, "STOP." Today, I choose to be different, and today, I show myself and the world that this day is given to be celebrated. This moment in time can be meaningful. I hope that as you're reading the words written in this work, in some small way, they shed light on you and give you endless hope that what you bring to the table is worth much. You will have no control over what others at that table accept from you. That is their problem, the issues they must deal with or be doomed to repeat. Some are quick to judge and pass sentence on to others while ignoring their own. Always allow them to think and say what they will. You will know better.

Be brave of heart and spirit. Walk where others are afraid to go. Lead the way, no matter your age, with the knowledge that you were created from the goodness you bring to us.

When I grew up, as a child, we yelled at each other when arguing; we did not know how to win. "Sticks and stones will break my bones, but words will never hurt me." The reality is that we were wrong in that saying. Words do hurt. Words incite actions that can harm us and those around us. Words can ruin a person's reputation, livelihood, and career. The words of a bully, someone who is set on making us a scapegoat, a target, can be devastating. That

is true with adolescents going through tremendous changes during their teen years.

A person can be reduced to tears. I recently read a statement a woman published about me, and it was a very hateful one, to say the least. Feelings that she and others felt about me. After the initial shock of seeing and reading those words, I allowed myself time to process what was written and where I am today. The woman knows nothing of my life today. It is her impression of who I am, but not who I am today.

Moreover, she has a right to her feelings, and I have the right to move on. If we allow that to happen, the past can weigh us down in the present. I chose to accept and hear what she had to say. I also choose not to deter who I am or what I can become. That is for each of us to decide when confronted by the words of another. We cannot simply dismiss them. We need to acknowledge what has been said and what it is based on and ask ourselves if we are now the person being described, criticized about, or plain hated.

The art of letting go is not refusing to recognize the truth but knowing what to do with that truth in light of many other facts. Our life is made up of so many moments and events that all must be put in perspective. We live in this moment, on this day. Yes, we all carry the baggage of the past. We all have known and unknown truths about us. The process of letting go and being free is learning how to put all those truths in their proper place. If it was true, then is it true today? And if it is not, we have to let go, not of the historical truth of that time, but of what we have done since that time. Growth is accomplished when we can see who we are right now.

What military personnel do during a time of war is not ordinary. Yet each man and woman who wears the uniform of their country has been trained to kill. To kill or be killed on the battlefield. Most of them hope or pray they never have to kill another person, but they prepare to do it if the need should arise. Letting go of those times can take years. Images, sounds, and screams often return at the least expected time. They can paralyze a person. A reality that too many of our citizens have to face when they return home to their respective families. Support systems are not always available. A form of life goes on, just not the life they had hoped for or expected years later.

Many people have lived with unreasonable employers, managers, or superiors. I was visiting a religious woman who was over one hundred years of age. We were talking in her room when she put her hand on my arm and said, "Remember this: Not everyone is good. I had some very bad superiors during my years in religious life, but I want you

to know, even though they are bad—God is good!"
She recounted how she watched those superiors
come and go. They did not like to be questioned or
challenged. They were harsh in their punishments,
but someone else replaced them after some time.
This sister was known for sneaking into their chapel
when she was supposed to be resting. Although
101 years of age, she would sit there, in front of the
Blessed Sacrament, and pray. Other times, she just
liked to sit there quietly and listen. She knew that
God already understood and had seen her life. So
just like two old friends who can sit on the sofa and
not say a word. Why should they, they already know
their friend, spouse, or lover? And this sister found
that just being there, in the presence of her God,
was more than sufficient and much better than lying
in bed resting. She knew how to let go of what was
harmful and hold onto what was necessary. I learned
a great deal from her. Mind you, she was not afraid to
tell me off when I was wrong. I recall one day, after
having lunch with a group of sisters, we were chat-
ting at the table about their life in Germany during
the time of the Second World War and Hitler. I
guess we talked too long because my dear old friend
suddenly said, "Enough talk; time to pray."

At that, the table of people broke apart, for we
knew she was right. A time to talk and a time for
silence. Finding the balance is not always as easy as it

sounds. However, if we realize our full potential and allow ourselves to grow despite what we might have gone through, we must have that silence. Reflective silence. It's not filled with background music or TV blaring, but it's quiet—the silence you find on a park bench, even in the city. You close your eyes and hear the birds chirping, dogs barking, and feet passing by as the wind gently blows your hair. A refreshing, reinvigorating gift given to be cherished for what it is. Our moment and time to relax, refresh, and revitalize ourselves is good. If we use those moments wisely, we discover that we can be free and alive—ready to take on whatever may come.

6

Titles, Roles, and Cockleshells

"Life is too short and too sweet to complain about the silly things" (**Michael Chandler**).

From an early age, we are taught to respect our elders. "Yes, ma'am" or "No, sir," not just "yea" or "nay." We call people by titles that we give them. I recall the first time my oldest niece came to the first high school that I was principal of and asked me why everyone kept calling me Father John when my name was Uncle Jack. She could not understand why they did not know who I was. I tried to explain that she was the only person in the world who could call me Uncle Jack because she was my niece.

My maternal grandfather was simply Gramp to me. Yet he was known within the community as Mr. Mayor. Elected to lead the largest land township within the state, he went from councilman to mayor over one long evening. I was old enough to understand what had taken place that election evening. On the other hand, my sister just knew this man to be Gramp.

In many cases, we call heads of departments Chief, not even using their sir name, just Chief, and everyone knows to whom our remarks refer. It is their position, their rank. The military has been doing this since there was a military. We address by rank. Someone yells, "General in the room," and everyone is up on their feet and saluting the figure walking into the room or down the aisle. We do not need to know their last name; the title elicits an instant response from those gathered. How often have we heard "Ladies and Gentlemen, the President of the United States," followed immediately by ruffles and flourishes being played, and there before us enters a neighbor, friend, and colleague, now and forever known as Mr. President?

Are not mom, dad, or mommy, daddy just titles we have given this man and woman once they become parents?

Individuals work hard to become CEOs, Chairman of the Board, University Presidents, or school Principals. People become more attentive, show respect, and keep their distance now that their positions and titles have changed. We are still the people we were the day before these new titles were given to us, but the perception of who we are changed instantly.

I recall all too vividly that after receiving my doctorate, a talk I had given at an affair, which might have cost $50–100. That same talk now brought in $300–500 to the university because "Doctor" was before my name, which presumably meant that I was more knowledgeable on the subject than I had been the week before. All that had changed was that a new title had been added, but my knowledge base remained the same. Perception is everything!

Stedman Graham said,

> Most people are defined by their titles, their cars, their house, where they came from, their color, their race, their religion. And so it's up to you to take control of your own life and define you. As long as you understand who you are and you have a solid foundation of understanding what your talents are, what your skills are.

Or as the TV character, Mr. Rodgers, taught us, "It's not the honors and not the titles and not the power that is of ultimate importance. It's what resides inside" (**Fred Rogers**).

We can easily forget that important lesson. We become so used to our title and our role in society that if you take it away from us, many find that they are lost as to what they are supposed to be and what they do now. Not being recognized in public can be very difficult for someone who has been identified for so long by their place and role within the community. It can lead to anxiety and depression. Getting up in the morning and seemingly having no purpose, no objective for the day. Who are they now? There are no longer expectations of what they should be doing. Influence is diminished, if not forgotten. Many individuals cannot accept being retired or no longer in the spotlight.

One of my friends has retired so often and returned to work that I have lost count of how many retirement parties he has been given. When confronted with an unstructured day, he finds nothing to fill those hours he would have been at his job. Retirement just did not fulfill him.

Another prominent figure, a Roman Catholic Bishop, told me that transitioning from the head of a diocese to becoming Bishop Emeritus was very difficult for him. Before, people had always invited him to attend one event or another. He was constantly asked out for dinner. Now, the phone no longer rang, inviting him over. He still had a secretary assigned to him, but fewer letters to dictate and sign.

He often sent letters to compliment or question an author about their book. I know; I received a few of those letters. I was surprised that he had read the latest book I published, and I was more surprised when he told me his favorite part was when I wrote about a particular area. Other times, it might have been to correct me whether he felt my take on something was off or not to his liking. At first, he did a good deal of reading. Then he found it did not fill in the whole day. It was a difficult transition from entering the office daily, being greeted by his secretary, who had all his appointments spelled out, and sitting at his desk. Now, the sheet of paper was nearly empty.

Wayne Dyer wrote, "Your life is like a play with several acts. Some of the characters who enter have short roles to play, others, much larger. Some are villains and others are good guys. But all of them are necessary; otherwise, they wouldn't be in the play. Embrace them all, and move on to the next act."

Our newspapers, especially online sites, enjoy poking fun at individuals. In most cases, politicians in this country and those of wealth and nobility in other countries. We allow it under the guise of free speech. In the Middle Ages, that form of mockery would probably demand someone lose their head over it.

Take, for example, a favorite children's rhyme: "Mary, Mary, Quite Contrary." We all recall how much of it goes, and maybe we even recited it ourselves as we grew up. It was directed at the daughter of Henry VIII—Mary. It seemed innocent, but it was far from being innocent.

When she became Queen of England, she ordered all to abandon the Church of England her father had started and return to the Roman Catholic Church. Her father had put Catholics who refused to become Protestant in prison or killed, and Mary followed his example by putting those who did not return to the Catholic faith to death. Recall the first part of the rhythm:

> Mary, Mary, quite contrary,
> How does your garden grow?
> With silver bells and cockleshells
> And pretty maids all in a row

It sounds so sweet yet is sinister in every line. Because the queen tried to erase much of what Henry VIII had implemented. She was considered to be difficult, well, outright contrary for a woman living in a man's world of power. Her garden grew from the blood shed by those who refused to follow her order and return to the Roman Catholic faith. And what about those beautiful silver bells and cockleshells? Again, the poem was written to mock the queen, not praise her.

In the medieval ages, silver bells were referred to as thumb screws. Metal devices were used on the prisoner who had their thumb forced inside. Then the metal was screwed down into the finger, bringing about horrific pain. Many individuals quickly recanted their Protestant faith and pledged to be Catholic again.

Cockleshells were equally devasting devices. They were created for one purpose: to cause genital torture to the person—male or female.

The people of her time were naturally enraged. There were mass protests and marches in the streets of London, but all to no avail. Her counselors all advised her to allow people to remain, but Mary, quite the contrary, refused to budge.

The cemeteries quickly filled up with newly executed men and women. This explains how your gardens grow—the result of using silver bells and cockleshells. And for those who did not succumb to the torture, Queen Mary introduced the guillotine. She had witnessed her former governess brutally having her head chopped off by an inept executioner who took eleven chops before he severed her head from her body. Mary believed the guillotine to be a milder way of performing executions, and thus, the people came to call it "the maiden" maid for short.

Therefore, the reference to pretty maids lined in a row referred to the guillotines and the crowd's pleasure in watching women having their heads chopped off more quickly and efficiently than in the past. The masses often taunted Queen Mary as she rode in her carriage with those simple words resonating through the crowd "Mary, Mary, quite contrary, how does your garden grow? With silver bells and cockleshells and pretty maids all in a row."

It is a most challenging lesson for those who are now in power, one often never learned. Whether elected to office, appointed, acquired by hereditary birth, or taken by force, all are accountable to the people. Those in power are not always right in their judgment or the execution of their office. They believe their words are above reproach. They are quick to silence those who question, especially in public, their decisions. Yet the people's voice is always stronger and mightier than those sitting on the proverbial throne.

How does the ordinary person or follower argue with God? Telling individuals and communities that it is God's will and that what I say or write is correct. Historically, religious leaders have been the worst. When they are hard-pressed, they fall back on God. As the Spirit works through them, for argument's sake, the Spirit of God works more profoundly and powerfully through the voice of the believers. The

Spirit of God is not limited to those in authority. And yet in most organized religious bodies, we find that the select few, in relation to the whole, are making the laws and issuing decrees that affect the lives of all. Right now, in churches worldwide, we see individual churches breaking communion with the central body over changes in doctrinal practices. Whether in the Church of England or the Methodist church at the corner of our street, the people say we have had enough. This is not what we believe; this is no longer the church we joined. They are choosing to go on their own. Whole dioceses, or congregations, are splitting from their communion with the universal church and taking a stand they believe to be correct. A church purifying itself. Central leaders may call them rebellious heretics, but the truth is that they are following their conscience as to what they hold the scriptures have directed them to follow.

Instead of listening to what is being said, religious leaders turn their backs, dig in, and proclaim their position to be true—foolery, at the least, and absolute pride at the worst. To think that these rebels know more of what God wants than those ordained or elected to lead know is beyond what they will tolerate. Yet before their eyes, the church as we know it is changing. Today's educated thinkers no longer need to be told what to do and how to live their lives. Yes, they look to the church for guidance, but they do not want to be treated as little children who need permission to follow their journey in life.

Power and fame may corrupt people. They begin to believe they have a right to be treated differently. In some way, they deserve treatment different from the entourage accompanying them. How many Secret Service agents will tell you how badly they were treated by the President of the United States or members of his family in their duty to protect them? How many men and women who work for leaders of countries, assemblies, and royalty tell us how they were never spoken to or ignored by their employer? Worse yet, they had to hide when their employer entered the room so they would not be seen. Or celebrities who demand what must be made available and what type of room they will stay in. What must be available to them as they wait for an interview to take place? How do they feel justified in trashing a hotel suite because they paid to use it?

Early on in my teaching career, one of the lessons I learned was that the most knowledgeable and informed individuals were not those in charge. Instead, the secretaries and custodial help were the most valuable resources within the school complex. Why? Simply because most people ignored them. They would come into the main office and never greet the secretary except to ask if her boss was in or available. Students, faculty, and administrators paid

no attention to the men and women who cleaned the
building every night, who walked the halls during
the day gathering trash and hearing hundreds of
conversations. These workers saw the writing on the
walls every day. They knew the pulse of the complex and knew when something was going down.
Yet no one spoke with them, and they were simply hired help. The cafeteria staff people were like
that also. They heard all those conversations taking
place as people chose what they wanted and chatted
with a colleague about what annoyed them that day.
Silent workers who took it all in. Yes, they talked
among themselves about what they heard and saw.
Sometimes, they even shared it with their supervi-
sor, who rarely, if ever, shared it with the administrators for fear of calling attention to the workers or
seeing them fired. In one school, I knew one hour
before the bomb call came in that it would happen.
A cleaner I had befriended stopped by my classroom
to warn me that I might be safer outside the building than inside. She had heard students talking as
she emptied the trash cans in the restrooms, saying that they planned to shut the school down and
show the administrators who were really in charge. I
thanked her for the warning and went down to the
Headmaster's and Academic Dean's offices and told
them what I believed to be accurate. Both looked
at me like I was out of my mind. I was politely dis-

missed and told there was no way they were shutting down the school or evacuating students based on some hearsay gossip.

I did not return to the classroom; instead, I went to the athletic fields and sat on the bleachers. Forty minutes later, the administrators received a call from the police to evacuate the building. A bomb threat had been called in, and they were on their way with dogs that would sniff out where the explosives were hidden if they were in the building. I heard the fire alarm go off and saw over a thousand people pour out of the buildings to their assigned areas as police cars, sirens blaring, came onto the property. Soon, officers and their specially trained canine assistants began the floor-by-floor search. An hour and a half later, all clear bell was sounded, twenty minutes before the day's last class was to end.

That evening, I stayed and thanked the cleaning lady as she was getting ready to go home. I took the time to thank each night person who was clocking in for their service and how one of them was so right in sharing what she had heard. I encouraged them to be vigilant; it was the 1970s, and war protests were taking place. Woodstock Musical Festival drew thousands who sang and danced to antiwar songs and ballads. It was not my job or place to thank them or encourage them to keep us informed. No, it was the responsibility of those who hired and paid them but rarely gave them the time of day. The administrators never mentioned the matter to me. I learned that my voice was nothing to them. I was just one of many teachers working in the complex.

When I was appointed as Principal of a high school, I was the youngest one they had in the system. Upon arriving at my new school, which I would be responsible for, I knew my first priority. I came during the summer break. Yes, school secretaries, as did all the custodians, still had to work. I called the woman who oversaw the dining hall and asked since I knew she and her staff were off for the summer, if she and some of her people would come in and prepare a luncheon for the secretaries, custodians, and themselves to have with me. She hesitated and asked me why. It had never been done in her ten years working there. I asked her to trust this unknown new principal and told her I would explain everything at the luncheon. Two days later, we all sat down to eat. Day and night shifts came in to meet and hear from me. At lunch, I told them I knew I was young enough to be one of their college graduates or grandchildren. They all laughed. But I told them I had learned how invaluable they were to be running this school. Yes, policy would be made by me. But they would know, way before I ever would, whether the new changes were being accepted or ignored. They would be the individuals who would sense the tenor of the place before any of us. We would all be caught up in our individual roles. I would need their valuable input.

The invisible are the most visible. Jesus said that those who have eyes to see cannot see. Those who have ears to hear cannot hear. It is true today as it was when first spoken. Some feel so important that they have no time for what others have to say, especially about them or their policies. Others use their position to intimidate and coerce others to do what they want to be done. A little bit of authority or power is always dangerous in the hands of those who have always sought it.

A new coach, teacher, or elected official is often caught up in their new position. They now must be listened to. Whether right or wrong, they are now in charge. Many times, they are easily offended when their decisions are questioned. I once had a math teacher who threw a sophomore out of class because he ate a piece of candy. The student argued with the teacher, who proceeded to lower his latest test grade from a B to a D. There was a written policy in the faculty handbook that clearly stated that grades could not be used as a means of discipline. All discipline issues were to be sent to the vice principal for student conduct, who would determine what, if any, punishment was called for.

This young man marched into my office, sat down in one of the chairs, looked straight at me, and said, "I thought you told us that if we did something wrong in class, it could not affect our grade but that we would be sent to the Vice Principal." I looked at the young man and told him he correctly recalled what I had shared. Grades were one thing; misbehavior was a discipline issue, and each was treated separately. He told me how the math teacher, in front of the class, went over and changed his grade as a punishment and then sent him out of the classroom. I left the student with the Vice Principal to handle the issue, and I went up to the classroom, knocked at the door, and asked the teacher to step out into the hall with me. When he did, and the door was closed, I asked if he had changed a student's test grade because the boy had eaten some candy and argued with him. He assured me he had done just that. I reminded him of the policy in the faculty handbook and asked him to return to the room and change the grade to a B. He told me it was his classroom and his students, and neither I nor the Vice Principal for Academics would tell him what to do in this domain. Once again, I asked him to reconsider and change the grade to what it was. When he refused, I entered the room, went over to his desk, and told the students that I was changing Shawn's test grade back to a B because that was what he scored. Grades were never to be used as a form of discipline in our school. I changed the grade, initialed it, and left the room to the teacher's fury.

That afternoon, the School's Administrative Council faculty representative confronted me on undermining a teacher, the authority of all teachers working here, by changing a student's grade without the teacher's approval. I asked the representative if the teacher had told him that I had asked the math teacher into the hall and asked him to follow the faculty handbook. He had refused twice to do that. It was only after the second refusal that I went in and changed the grade and reminded the students that grades and discipline were two distinct things in this school. The representative told me that the teacher had forgotten to mention that. He only told their representative how I had burst into his room and proceeded to embarrass him by changing the grade without his consent. I agreed that he had not consented but that he clearly had violated the faculty policy and that the academic Vice-Principal would write the reprimand up and have it inserted into his file. The elected representative apologized and agreed that I had followed protocol, given him ample opportunity to do it himself, and that he would face the consequences of his actions. There would be nothing further from the rest of the faculty regarding this matter.

Titles and roles mean little in life, except for the ego of the person holding them, if they are not used for improving, elevating, and strengthening the lives of those we work and live with daily. All authority is there for the welfare of the whole. The higher the position or title, the greater the responsibility to listen first, speak slowly, and serve the needs of those with no voice in policymaking. If they cannot do that, we should vote them out of office and remove them from their position of authority as unworthy.

If we are to be free, we must let go of false ideas of what authority is and of those who exercise it. We are the governed. Their jurisdiction and position come from us. When we approve of their appointment or election, you and I are their natural power source. But we are not imbecilic, indentured servants or sheep that follow heedlessly wherever we are led. No, each of us has a dignity that is our own and has nothing to do with our position. Each of us has a vision of life, where we should be going, and how to get there that needs to be heard, acknowledged, and respected. There is no place for the timid in such circumstances. We cannot be frightened by their intimidation of us, their veiled threats of what might happen if we do not adhere to what they want. It is said that no man is an island. Never allow yourself to be so pushed, coerced, and manipulated that you are dismissed and ignored as if you do not count. It is not only your voice that needs to be heard; it is you, the individual, different from the one next to you, that must be embraced.

Everyone must be respectfully heard in large workplaces, institutions, schools, communities, and even our home life. Children have a voice that cannot be dismissed because they are children. What do they know? Suppose we ignore their suggestion or ideas at that age. In that case, we send a clear message to them of their value—intentionally or unintentionally. They learn quickly that their voice is of little importance. And yet how many times have we not heard adults say, "Out of the mouth of babes," the truth is spoken? They tell us what is accurate because it is all they know. They have not learned to nuance their words, sugarcoat the ugly truth, or lie but answer the question they were asked—a vital lesson for all adults to remember if we earnestly want to be free.

7

What Is Important to You?

The longer we live, what is important to us changes. What was important when you were a teenager and ready to enter the workforce or start college?

Do you still believe the things you pursued then are essential to you? Were they ever really that important to begin with within the picture of who you are today? Ambition, a desire to make a difference, to change what we saw all around us, might have ruled our day in our late teens and early twenties. We would learn that change comes slowly, if at all. Unfortunately, we would learn to play the game at work, at home, and in our communities. Otherwise, we would soon be labeled rebels, troublemakers who should be avoided at all costs.

We learn many hard lessons as we grow older. If we were accustomed at home or school to being respected and heard out, we quickly knew in the

workforce or first-year college that virtually everyone else felt the same way or had the same experience
before this point. We were now one voice among
many. Once again, we would have to present ourselves, our ideas, and our vision to men and women
with equally strong views. Some of us plunged into
the fray and tried to make our mark on this new
world we entered. Others, being overwhelmed, either
dropped out or quietly fell into the background and
observed.

I can recall feeling lost at times during the first
weeks in college. No one from my family had ever
had the opportunity to attend college. I was the first.
Here I was in the midst of a sea of strangers. We
were trying to find the right building that housed
the class we were supposed to attend at this time
of day. We first-year students ran from building to
building, hoping to be at the next class on time. And
why, in heaven's name, did it always seem to be so far
away from the one I was just in? Amazingly, we all
survived those first weeks, learned where we had to
be, and found the campus smaller than we thought
the first week we wandered about. We also began to
trust one another and start new friendships.

I learned I had a northern accent from students
from southern states. I indeed knew that they had
accents. We learned to laugh about how we sounded
to one another. All my life, eighteen years, I thought

everyone sounded like me or those I grew up around. We began to learn about cultural differences and ethnic ones as a new world unfolded in the classroom, dorms, playing fields, and free time. People talked for hours, over a cup of coffee or soda pop, about world issues, issues in our country, or the communities we came from. It was a world I both envied and enjoyed. I was changing from a naïve young man to a more knowledgeable man who knew he did not know much about many subjects. And that was okay. That is why we are where we are at this moment in time. Professors sharing their knowledge and, in many cases, wisdom gained over years of communicating with students like us. We learned from one another that it was all right to admit that we did not know what the blazes the professor had talked about that day. Someone in the room did, and we pounced on one another as we begged them to explain what he spoke of that day. I will gladly admit that a glass or pitcher of beer always helped us communicate better as we sat around the table at the local pizza store.

The reality is, as we age, what is significant changes. I often laugh when reporters ask politicians to defend something they said or wrote twenty-five or more years ago. When they try to say, over those years, they have evolved, and their understanding of the issue is different today than it was at that time long ago. If we are not constantly looking at positions we have taken and issues we fought over and are willing to admit that we may have been wrong or did not appreciate all that was involved, we have become stagnant. Jesus used to call people like that whitewashed tombs. Pretty on the outside but stinking on the inside. Stagnation leads to both intellectual and psychological demise. Knowledge is fluid. Our life is fluid. To attempt to keep everything the way it was is not moving forward.

Any company or corporation content to rely on past products or services and not explore new ways to serve their clients or followers is doomed to cease. We should celebrate what brought us to this place in time, learn from what proved to touch the lives of others, and find new ways to bring forth the best we can. Our personal life is no different. We let go of what was and seek what can be, or we are like people running for hours on a treadmill and going nowhere in reality. Yes, we will burn off fat and strengthen our hearts, but what good is it if I continue to do the same old stuff the rest of the day and not seek new ways to improve myself, the vision of the world that I have, and how as an individual I can bring that about. We cannot continue to use others as a crutch for our inability to take responsibility. Whether good or bad, we are responsible for what comes out of our mouths and what we have done. We might not be proud of all that has happened, and we may deeply regret words and deeds, but historically, they are all part of our history. It is what we make of that history and how it shapes our future insights and actions into future stances.

Think about all the people you know. Most of us can place them in one of three categories. There is the pessimistic type who only sees risk at every new venture, all the reasons why something should not be introduced, and that everything is fine the way it has been for ages. Then we know men and women who look at what is as—realists. They neither see what has been as a value that cannot change, nor do they look to the future to solve all the issues they face today. For them, today has enough problems, and they are happy to address and tackle them now. Finally, we have associates and friends who are dreamers. Yes, they know that today has problems unique to this time, but they keep looking forward to what could be if we all worked toward that goal. They are the ones who always present new ways of looking at and moving forward to a new vision fit for this time and into the next generation. And yes, some of us do not fit into any of those categories. We are still determining what we want, when we want it, or how to get it.

When we have serious discussions about issues that have come up and have to be addressed, we need individuals who represent the above three categories at the table. It will slow the process down as we listen to the views of one another. Still, in the end, we will have heard what the worst-case scenario is, what is the most reasonable for right now, and what our decision could mean for them, not just now, but in the future and the direction we want to go.

Unfortunately, those in authority usually surround themselves with like-minded individuals. People they can trust and know they share a like vision. Sometimes, we call them "yes men/women" because they readily agree with the head of the organization, corporation, institute, or church leader. There is no honest discussion, objection, or ability to challenge the direction we are going or being taken toward for fear of displeasure or being removed from our position at the table. At that moment, a bell should ring in our heads, reminding us that we just relinquished our voice, freedom, and that of many others by simply agreeing.

Letting go is an art. Every artist knows they cannot keep producing the same works if they intend to make a decent living. Look throughout history at the artists we admire whose works still inspire, challenge, and bring about a sense of awe in us years after their death. They keep drawing from within themselves to bring about the subsequent work inside them, buried until now. You and I are no different.

Most of us have yet to begin to tap into everything we have stored away over the years. Everything we have seen, heard, and lived through has been stored away. Hopefully, it will be brought forth at the right time and place.

Is yesterday more important than today? Do you find that your mind dwells more on things that have happened already or on what they can be? When we were young, we dreamt of all we would or could do once we were on our own. Living life as we believed it should be lived. Dreams of what can be filled our heads. More important would be our ability to do the work necessary to bring them about. That is the challenge we face. Many would meet too many obstacles to see their dream become reality. Others would see it happen. But at what price? What did they have to do to bring it about? Did the dream have a cost that was more than one could bear?

We can try to cover that pain using legally prescribed or illegal drugs. We can rely on alcohol to dull or blur what was and now brings us into a drunken state night after night.

Then there is a way to look back, accept all that has been, and take this time to make a new history of our lives. Every seven years, our body physically changes. We are constantly shedding particles of skin—human dander. I would suggest we also take time to clear what was negative, the failures we experienced, and the harm that was done, and allow this time in our lives to be different. We are always the center of our historical reflection. We can build on what good we know and, with the same determination, allow the negative happenings to be historical. These next hours of our lives will enable us to become more than we were yesterday. We need to lay a stronger foundation for what we can still be as members of society and a voice to be heard.

Many faiths hold that we reflect a divine origin. My faith proclaims that we were created in the image of our God. We were created as good. We were created equal, whether man or woman. We were challenged to grow, to take control of the world around us, and to take care of it and all life on the planet. From the start of human existence, the care of the Earth was entrusted to us. The well-being of one another was equally assigned to each one of us. These are things that should be important to us. Instead of constantly seeking what gives us pleasure or momentary satisfaction, we should be looking outside of ourselves at the bigger picture of which we are a part.

As mentioned earlier, we, if you will, are part of a great puzzle. All the pieces lie before us to be arranged and rearranged until we see the puzzle brought together as a whole. You and I are single pieces in that puzzle, but it always remains incomplete without us. When we ignore or fail to embrace all whom we encounter, we are, in fact, destroying that puzzle. We limit our own ability to see the beauty that can be and is just waiting for us to bring it about. Yes, some pieces are as dull as can be, but they are still a part of the beauty of the whole. How many puzzles have you done with endless skies or fields or oceans? We struggled to make sense of them when they were just individual pieces forming a larger image. That is, until the day you placed the final piece of the puzzle into place, stood back, and looked at what was done. Only then do we see the fruit of our labor, the magnificence of all those individual pieces, now in their rightful place making the whole look great.

Take time to seriously look around you this week. Look at all the different faces; do not just see them, but really look at them. Look at the person who belongs to that face and begin to appreciate that they are all individually different from you. And it is that diversity that does not separate us from one another but, in truth, brings us together as a whole. It enriches us and makes us stretch our notions of what should be from what is. We grow in relation to how well we can accommodate those differences and accept them for who they are while celebrating who we are and what we bring to the community each new day.

Children worldwide know these words written by the **Sherman Brothers** for the Disneyland boat ride of that same name, which sums up what we need to remind ourselves of at the start of each new day.

> It's a world of laughter, a world
> Of tears
> It's a world of hopes and a
> World of fears
> There's so much that we share
> That it's time we're aware
> It's a small world, after all.

What should be important to all of us is how we make this small planet of ours a better world, how we enhance the lives of all those that inhabit this Earth, and how we improve the quality of our air, waters, and vegetation. The Boy Scouts have a motto of leaving a site in better shape than they found it. Should we, not all, strive to do that for the generations that follow us? Our dreams may not have come to pass as we thought they would. We can make dreams possible for those who follow in our steps. We either learn from our collective history or ignore lessons learned or missed opportunities. Our constant challenge is not to miss opportunities given to us to make a difference, as small as they might be. We can still dream of what can be—it is a small world, after all.

8

Set Us Free

Maya Angelou stated, "It's one of the greatest gifts you can give yourself, to forgive. Forgive everybody."

And that is where we start our journey of being free to live, love, celebrate, and perform to our full potential. I will admit it is much easier said than done. It takes real effort and work on our part. The hurt and the anger have been with us for much too long. In many ways, our vision of others has been tainted by our experiences or life-changing events. Yet to be free, it has to start somewhere—no better place than within us. We do not need to look further than our own hearts and spirit. When that rope of pain no longer shackles our heart, and our soul is not being dragged down by memories we have not been able to let go of before now, we will remain bound to those moments in the past—historic moments in life's journey, but moments that have now passed.

From history, we learn. We comprehend better what is good and what is evil. What limits our ability to dance freely in celebration of who we are?

Now is the time for us to learn new dance steps. We leave behind two left feet and find our footing and gracefulness again. I believe it was **Marianne Williamson** who told us, "Forgiveness is not always easy. At times, it feels more painful than the wound we suffered, to forgive the one that inflicted it. And there is no peace without forgiveness."

"You can't forgive without loving. And I don't mean sentimentality. I don't mean mush. I mean having enough courage to stand up and say, 'I forgive. I'm finished with, it" (**Maya Angelou**). And when we can truly do that, we put our foot down and begin our new dance steps. It will be step-by-step. But each new step releases part of our past and takes us in a new direction. Like any dance, there is a mystery to those steps. Any dancer will tell you it is not the individual steps taken, all of them being necessary; it is the whole routine that produces beauty and "awes and wows" from the spectators of the dance.

Life is like a great choreography. We may stumble through it, even fall flat on our faces, but we get up again and try again to master what the director of the choreography has shown us must be done.

The **Rev. Dr. Martin Luther King Jr.** preached, "We must develop and maintain the capacity to forgive. He who is devoid of the power to forgive is devoid of the power to love. There is some good in the worst of us and some evil in the best of us. When we discover this, we are less prone to hate our enemies." Time after time, being physically beaten, arrested, and verbally abused, he demonstrated that statement to the world and those who followed him in establishing a more just and equal society where all people, no matter their race, color, or origin, could walk side by side in a uniform step to new freedom. It is that determination and belief that what has been does not have to be what allows any of the hope of making change that transforms us and those around us. We are all called to make our planet a better place than what we inherited. Likewise, family relationships, community relationships, and commitments can also change and grow. The steps to this dance, this new freedom that allows us to whirl around the room in movements unseen, unknown before we were present, is our challenge.

As I share with you, I recall King Louis XIV. When Versailles was almost finished being built, he was not finished transforming royal life, the life of the nobility, and the whole of France. At one point, he created and introduced to the court a new dance he had made. Step-by-step, he slowly danced around the room as the music was being played. He was caught up in the moment, the beauty of the dance, and wanted the whole court to learn it, dance it, and share in his excitement. Because he was king, no one dared to object. The men and the women of the court slowly entered the ballroom floor and began to follow the steps of their king. Before the night was over, it is said most of those present knew enough to join in the dance's beauty.

Do not allow your two left feet to stop you. Nor let that walker or wheelchair hold you back. Listen to the music in your heart. Listen to the beat and imagine your movement across the floor. Allow yourself not to be shackled by memories of the past but what this moment can be for you. To be fully alive, we must learn how to let go.

Jodi Picoult reminds us, "When you're different, sometimes you don't see the millions of people who accept you for what you are. All you notice is the person who doesn't."

When King Louis danced alone, creating his new waltz, many a servant probably thought he had lost his mind. He understood who he was—the Sun King—and soon, people would dance around ballroom floors thanks to the imagination and determination of this king.

What we need to grow to move forward is already within us. Our challenge is to draw from depths we have not explored before. We must believe that there was a reason for our being when we were born. No other will be like us. We sometimes get lost in all those around us and believe they are wiser, more competent, and more equipped than us. The truth is that we are endowed with an innate ability to see outside ourselves. Possibly, as we grew up, we were not allowed to articulate or share what we felt or believed. Maybe we were silenced too often and finally just stopped trying. But now is our time to be alive, to follow our inner dance.

Lou Holtz famously said, "You were not born a winner, and you were not born a loser. You are what you make yourself be."

Every woman and man need to be heard. Whether young or old, their voice must still be recognized, heard, and considered. Many older individuals feel, because of their age and disability, that they no longer should speak up. Just let the younger members of the group and the community speak since they will be the ones taking over. Instead of forgetting about them, we should solicit their input from the experiences they have had and are having even now. Are they being marginalized because of age or disability? Every voice is essential if growth is to take place. What one of us misses, another sees. What a person cannot articulate clearly, another can add their voice for clarity. We build on one another.

We strive and grow as all members feel valued, and their work, words, and life are vital.

We let go of that, which tied us down. We dance to a new beat and raise our voices in a new song. Christians believe they are created in the image of their God. Then let the voice of God be heard by our words. These are simple words, but they are always profound because they come forth from our very soul. Every person is not educated the same way, but each is educated. My grandmother always told me that she graduated from the school of hard knocks. She learned much over the ninety-three years of her life. She just wanted to be heard at this time, in this place, by this family. And she listened to what we all had to share. Not that she always agreed, but we knew she always heard us, which was enough. She earned the title of matriarch of the family.

I grew up in a family where our grandparents and great-grandparents were alive. Many families I know do not have that experience. It enriched my life to know them and listen to them tell their stories, from when they came to the United States to the present day and all they had seen and experienced. My great-grandmother was baptized a Presbyterian. One day, when I was over at my grandparents' house, she was in her room. As I passed by, I saw her praying the rosary. I stopped, knocked on the door frame, and asked if I could come in. She waved me in. I asked her why she was praying the rosary and where she learned how to pray it. She learned it from the TV. where she watched a show of sisters who prayed it each day. Nana found the repetition of Hail Marys peaceful and a source of closeness to God. She told me that there were many roads a person could follow to get to God. If this helped her, she knew God would not mind this Presbyterian praying it daily. Her voice needed to be heard by me, and she needed to be recognized and celebrated. It was a precious moment shared by an equally special Swedish lady.

I encourage each person to walk into a room, knowing that something would be lost if you were not there among these other individuals. When someone asks what you think, speak up loud and clear. Your voice is important, and it is one that all should hear. And if they forget to ask you, get their attention, and share it anyway. Never let an opportunity go by without your contribution. "Consult not your fears but your hopes and your dreams. Think not about your frustrations, but about your unfulfilled potential. Concern yourself not with what you tried and failed in, but with what it is still possible for you to do" (**Pope John XXIII**).

Or on entering a gathering of people, many of whom we know too well, we can take the advice of **St. Teresa of Avila** when she penned these words: "God has been very good to me, for I never dwell upon anything wrong which a person has done, so as to remember it afterwards. If I do remember it, I always see some virtue in that person."

Virtually every major religious belief system has proclaimed to its followers that they came into this world good. No one is born evil. It is that goodness we seek to find, to allow it to shine or free them from their past baggage and enable them to dance. I am that person; you are that person as we walk into a room. We have nothing to fear because we are better than all our failures. Some will throw the past into your face or whisper it as you pass by. At that moment, you push your shoulder back; you raise your head high, thank them for sharing their feelings, and tell them you forgive them. It is the one thing they cannot do: Forgive you or let go of their anger or hatred. That is their burden to carry; it is no longer yours.

"What lies behind us and what lies before us are tiny matters compared to what lies within us" (**Ralph Waldo Emerson**).

The great comedian **W. C. Fields** said, "It ain't what they call you. It's what you answer to."

Our freedom lies right inside of us. As we accept who we are and what has occurred throughout our lives, we correct what was wrong, put behind us what bound us to the past, and accept who we are now and what we can still become; we are free. **Voltaire** wrote, "God gave us the gift of life; it is up to us to give ourselves the gift of living well."

Recently, I came upon, in my reading, this quote: "Beginning today, treat everyone you meet as if they were going to be dead by midnight. Extend to them all the care, kindness and understanding you can muster, and do it with no thought of any reward. Your life will never be the same again" (**Og Mandino**).

It sounds radical, maybe even harsh, when you read those words. But if we knew that before the day was out, would we really be arguing, demanding, or harassing this person? Most rational beings would not. We would not want that to be the last remembrance we have of today's encounter. Being free also means setting free. We cannot continue trying to control, manipulate, or force others to our point of view. Living in the moment, not the past nor the future, dictates that we enter into life-giving conversations, negotiations, discussions, or policymaking as if what we say and do this day is all people will remember us by. When you get ready to retire tonight, spend a few moments thinking about how others around you will recall you. Will they recall the stubborn, pigheaded, obstinate individual who shot down everything anyone had to say that did not agree with their vision? Or will they remember at your funeral someone who listened, heard the views of others, and was willing to modify their position for the good of the whole? Believe me, you or I could easily be dead by nightfall.

Nothing planned by us, but we get hit by a vehicle as we cross the street. Or our car leaves the icy or wet-soaked road, rolls down an embankment, or slams into another object. A fire starts while we sleep, engulfing us before we can exit. Or simply, we drop dead. Death comes, and remembrances begin. We lost so many family members and friends to COVID before we had time to say goodbye. People lose their lives to unexpected flooding that overtakes their houses and towns. Life goes on, but for those who got caught up in any of those tragic moments, there are just the remembrances of those who lived.

William James said, "The greatest discovery of my generation is that a human being can alter his life by altering his attitude."

Norman Vincent Peale said, "Watch your manner of speech if you wish to develop a peaceful state of mind. Start each day affirming peaceful, contented and happy attitudes and your days will tend to be pleasant and successful."

Kahlil Gibran wrote, "Your living is determined not so much by what life brings to you as by the attitude you bring to life; not so much by what happens to you as by the way your mind looks at what happens."

Every time we change our attitude, alter our perception of what is happening, and affirm the good that can be, we take one more step toward our freedom. The more accessible we are, the more we can empower others to be free. It is always the insecure individual who demands others adhere to their way. They create more rules, regulations, and laws to ensure others conform.

To dance to your own music and celebrate life as an individual and a member of a family, community, corporation, or country call for a freedom that allows all of us to be different. I do not suggest that organized groups will not have specific demands for their members or followers. But those demands must reflect the reality of those they are meant to help, serve, and protect.

9

Free to Be

"Being young isn't about age. It's about being a free spirit. You can meet someone of 20 who's boring and old, or you can meet someone of 70 who's youthful and exciting. I met Fred Astaire when he was 72 and I was 21, and I fell in love with him. He certainly was a free spirit" (**Twiggy**).

No matter our present age, let us not allow the number of years to limit what we still can be. It is true that as the years pass and we age, our bodies and sometimes our minds begin to give out on us. We find we are more prone to losing our balance, remembering what we did yesterday or where we put our umbrellas or car keys. We do not recall names as quickly as we once did but give us a moment or two, and we may remember. If we are starting to enter the workforce, we may find that not everyone sees life the way we do. We may even find that some senior staff made it to that position because they gave freely of themselves over the years. They contributed daily, and those contributions made a difference. In your youthful exuberance to make your mark, never forget it is you, the whole package, who have been hired. As we saw in previous chapters, we all bring a perspective, a vision of life, work, fellowship, and ethics that might be good for those we now work with or live with daily. Only when we forget who we are in relationship to the person standing next to us are we no longer an asset. We do not need to conform for the sake of conforming. Nor is it necessary to be the rebel, the troublemaker, to be heard. We are listened to because we have something to say. We bring insight from our unique experiences and long or short journeys. It is what lies within us that must be brought forth. Once we have dealt with our demons, fears, and weaknesses and accepted who we are, we become genuine contributors to this place, these individuals, while remaining true to ourselves.

Previously, we talked about the ability to dance to a new tune, to create steps and movements that feel right to us, and simultaneously give pleasure. **Drew Barrymore** expressed that sentiment: "A few years ago, I bought an old red bicycle with the words Free Spirit written across the side—which is exactly what I felt like when I rode it down the street in a tie-dyed dress."

Something so simple as riding a bike, with the wind blowing in our hair, lifting our spirit as we pedal along and observe all around us. Or lying in the tub, filled with bubbles and some Epsom salts for those aches and pains, allows us to drift away, to be free, for a little while as our body becomes rejuvenated and refreshed. Maybe just getting out, walking, or running allows us to feel the adrenaline pump through our limbs, freeing those tense muscles, letting us let go and smile at all that stressed us. Being free does not have to cost us monetarily; it is always before us to be grasped, appreciated, and held onto this gift of freedom.

As we appreciate our newfound freedom from what held us back in the past, we find ourselves compelled to pass it on. We do not live in isolation; we are members of all types of communities. Take to heart the words **Maya Angelou** spoke, "The truth is, no one of us can be free until everyone is free." We all should feel that pain when one of us continues to hurt. A pain we have known in our own lives and can see in the eyes of another.

Franklin D. Roosevelt once said, "Human kindness has never weakened the stamina or softened the fiber of a free people. A nation does not have to be cruel to be tough."

Our strength is finding ways to set others free of all that holds them from fulfilling their destiny. A kind word, an embrace, an ear that listens and not just hears the words, a tissue to wipe tears away, the gift of forgiveness where hurt has been. All this is within our power. It costs us some time, empathy, care, and love, but it can delight the receiver greatly. That becomes an integral part of recovery. The ability we now have to share with others what they need at this moment is a continued part of our recovery. Hearing their voice—both spoken and unspoken— allows us to show them the attention they deserve, the care they need, the embrace that says so much. Living in the light is much healthier and better than living in darkness. As we feel freer about ourselves, we can help others experience that same sense of freedom from whatever it was that has continued to darken their lives. Virtually all those around us have their demons, character flaws, hurts, and scars that, unless addressed, always get in the way at the most unexpected moments. That is why many of the topics and suggestions in the first part of this book are essential in our lives if we are going to be fully available to those we find ourselves able to help. Let us look at that from a different perspective. **Les Brown** put it this way: "In every day, there are 1,440 minutes. That means we have 1,440 daily opportunities to make a positive impact."

"Positive thinking is more than just a tagline. It changes the way we behave. And I firmly believe that when I am positive, it not only makes me better, but it also makes those around me better" (**Harvey Mackay**).

Or "When you show deep empathy toward others, their defensive energy goes down, and positive energy replaces it. That's when you can get more creative in solving problems" (**Stephen Covey**).

Without realizing our impact on others, we can be a reason for them to celebrate this day, this moment, and maybe even life itself. There is endless beauty all around us; it is being able to let go of all the business of the day, all the things we have to do that cannot wait, that holds all of us from being free to see what is truly important. If, in the next minute, you or I have a heart attack, all those things that needed to get done, that could not wait, would come to a screening halt. Maybe they would not be done today, but I can assure you that another would pick up the ball and go about getting them done. We are not so significant or necessary that someone else cannot replace us. We might believe we are that important, but history shows we are not. There is always another out there who will do everything we prize about our ability. And they might even do it better than you or I ever could. I believed I was doing essential work others were not trained for or ready to do. How wrong I was. When removed from the picture by circumstances I brought about, many stepped in and continued the work at hand.

A mother often feels the family would fall apart if she were not taking them to soccer practice, cheerleading, cooking for them, or being present for their activities. A dad takes on overtime all too often, believing that without the money it brings in, his family will not be able to have all they want. Maybe they will not be able to have all they want. Still, his presence at home, being an integral part of their life and activities, may be much more important than the new Nikes, the new car, or the house he provides for them.

When we are free enough to acknowledge our limitations, skills, and achievements, will we be able to let go of what stops us from being happy at the end of the day? We go to bed all too often, dissatisfied with ourselves or our work that day. Always believing we could have done more. When in truth, our body, mind, and spirit were telling us to slow down and do less but more important things for body, mind, and spirit.

"Having a positive mental attitude is asking how something can be done rather than saying it can't be done" (**Bo Bennett**).

Or as **Charles R. Swindell** wrote, "We cannot change our past. We can not change the fact that people act in a certain way. We can not change the inevitable. The only thing we can do is play on the one string we have, and that is our attitude."

It is what we bring to every discussion, every planning session, and every decision we are asked to participate in. Turning a negative discourse into a positive one or simply embracing the negative is possible. If we have made the necessary changes in our own lives and confronted all our weaknesses or demons, what we now bring is not negative energy to the room. Still, we bring the possibility of seeing what might be missing. Not what we did in the past, nor judging those who went before us, but showing those we are now engaged with how each of us can contribute to a healthier, more stable, and satisfying situation for those we are responsible for. It is not a question of criticizing what is on the table but instead pointing out what we can add that makes it easier to accept, live with, and grow by. If growth is not a part of any planning, that lies with us. We are at these discussions for a reason. We were not asked to participate because we were perceived as having nothing of value to share. No, we were and are there because we have something important to bring. We bring our newfound freedom, our vision of a better self, a better work environment, and a better world. That is indeed something we can celebrate each day. We see life and situations differently and allow others to do the same. It is then that real progress is made in difficult situations, negotiations, and problem-solving sessions. Never underestimate what one voice in the midst of other voices can do; if that voice is filled with confidence, assurance, respect, and acceptance, it will be heard.

Although we may share common goals and objectives, the work lies in how we reach them and implement them. Here is where each of our voice's counts. Usually, we are given a copy of what a group of peers believes should be the way to achieve our end. Remember, it is one way, which means other ways can still be explored and worked into the pages we are confronted with. Our individual experiences, whether good or bad in the past, now come into play. Are our own experiences as members expressed in this document? Are the excellent points built upon or even acknowledged? Are those that were not productive or helpful for you or others being changed, or is this the time to challenge them? If the thought crosses your mind, it probably is time to speak up, write your comments and reasons, and pass them on.

As you know, even painful change does not occur in a void. Someone must put light on the issue for others to see what you have seen, experienced, and lived through. If it happened to us as we lived with these individuals, we could be reasonably confident that others have experienced the same thing as we did. Since we have confronted our demons and weaknesses and called them out for what they were in our lives and how they hindered our growth and development, we must share that so others may be freed of unnecessary ways of living, thinking, and celebrating.

It is somewhat like entering a new year. We set for ourselves particular goals that we would like to achieve. Maybe we want to exercise more, lose weight, cut back, or stop smoking, drinking, or drug use.

First, we articulate for ourselves what we want to do, possibly share it with others, and then go about the heroic task of trying to implement what we want. Maybe we only keep at it for a few weeks or months, possibly only days before we give up. But each year, we try again, dreaming about what could be. It is part of living and growing. We check off things accomplished and allow the others to wait for another day or time. It is the normal flow of life, like sitting on the beach and watching the waves come in and out rising majestically, thundering down, and pulling back to do it repeatedly. The ocean continually renews itself, and so must we. We need both the highs and lows to be fully alive, fully human.

We cry, and we laugh. We fall, and we get up. We stumbled but regained our footing. We are simple men and women on a life journey. We must never forget that it is a life journey. We build on experiences; we learn from failed ones and hopefully correct those. But move on, we do. We have much to be grateful for every day. The mere fact that we get to celebrate another day is a gift in itself. Oh, maybe it will not be an outstanding day or may turn out to be a miserable day, but we know that by comparing it to what has gone before. In twenty-four hours, we will start again. Allow those feet to embrace each new day with a new dance step, a lighter step. Even if you find yourself bedridden this day, move those toes, stretch your legs as best you can, and clap your hands for this new hour given. A simple smile costs nothing when someone comes to see us but is always welcomed and inviting.

When I was a young teacher, I remember a former student saying that he always knew what kind of visit it would be when he stopped by simply by the way I greeted him. If I shook his hand, it would be somewhat formal, to the point time spent before I would send him off, but if I embraced him, he knew we would laugh, share endless stories, and be at peace with one another. At the time, I never realized I was so easy to read by those who knew me. We live; we learn. People read us better than we read ourselves at times. That is why it is so essential that we make every effort to understand what we can change, what we can do to improve our quality of life, and how to live comfortably in our own skin. Once we do accomplish that, we can just be ourselves. Amazingly, you will discover that more individuals embrace you at that point than before. They will find in you a person who is at ease, easy to chat with, share with, and be with or around. In you, they will discover it is okay to acknowledge and even laugh at our eccentricities. To be alive is to accept who and what you are entirely.

Brandon Jenner said, "We can bring positive energy into our daily lives by smiling more, talking to strangers in line, replacing handshakes with hugs, and calling our friends just to tell them we love them." When was the last time, if at all, you energetically did those things?

Put more simply, as **Maria Montessori** wrote, "Free the child's potential, and you will transform him into the world." Who says we all must color within the lines? How many famous artists of our day have indeed proved through their works of art that there are no boundaries to creativity, expression, or fulfillment? So forget the lines that constrict, think outside the box, and embrace that which is to be. How does someone like Michelangelo look at a solid block of marble and clearly see David inside it? All he had to do was chip away until one of the great masterpieces of all time stood for everyone to see what he saw in the block of marble. I encourage everyone to be a chipper, not just a looker. Explore, tinker, and play with ideas, materials, music, and life itself. We have this one life to live—live it as if it meant something to us that we want to share with others and leave as a legacy.

A favorite person of mine wrote, "Birds sing after a storm; why shouldn't people feel as free to delight in whatever sunlight remains to them" (**Rose Kennedy**).

Stand in the light of a new day. Do not allow darkening clouds to blur your vision of what this day can be about. Today, you can walk with a quicker step and a more determined purpose in your stride—because you are fully alive!

> The free soul is rare, but you know it when you see it—basically because you feel good, very good, when you are near or with them. (**Charles Bukowski**)

> In life, if you don't know the truth, then you can't be free, because then you'll believe that the lies are the truth. But once we realize that when we read the Word of God, and you know the truth of who you are, then I'm not a man

without arms and legs. I am a child
of God. (**Nick Vujicic**)

Or we could echo the words of **Swami Vivekananda**, "The moment I have realized God sitting in the temple of every human body, the moment I stand in reverence before every human being and see God in him—that moment I am free from bondage, everything that binds vanishes, and I am free."

Ralph Waldo Emerson famously said, "It is not length of life, but depth of life."

It does not matter how many years or days we live here on this planet; what you and I add to life, the Earth, and issues of humanity is what matters.

I cannot count the number of times in my life when the phone rang, and I was being told that someone I cared about, someone who I worked with or loved, was dying, and I needed to come or had just died, and the family needed me now. It did not matter whether the call came at home or while I was away on vacation or visiting—it always meant that this was not my time but time to be with someone else. It is time to sit at a bedside, hold hands with this person, and give them the freedom to go—to be free of the last constraints that bind them to this existence. To watch them grasp in the air for those they loved and can now only see before them, invisible to my eyes, but clear as the rising sun to them.

I told the man who worked for me and coached some of our school's teams that it was all right for him to leave. He asked me if his two Italian sisters knew and if his wife knew he was dying. I assured him I had just spoken with his sisters, who carried on like there would be no tomorrow, and his wife, who just shook her head that it was time. That night, around eight thirty, his wife called to tell me she was at the hospital and that her husband had died, and she never knew it until his hand became cold in hers. Silently, gently, he had left us and completed his journey in peace. The church was filled at his funeral with those he taught for over forty-some years or the men he coached for about the same time. All came because one man had touched their lives and made them a better person as a result. It was not the length of his days they recalled but who the man was. In other words, the depth of life he lived had helped them realize they had much to give, as he had given himself to them.

Before I left the hospital that day, he called me back and asked me to bend down next to him as he lay on his bed. And so I did. He grabbed my head and kissed me on each cheek, tears running down his face. He thanked me for telling him the truth, for being there for him when he needed me the most, and that those kisses were the last sign of friendship and love, he would share with me. I cried as I drove back home that afternoon, so long ago.

Emma Bombeck stated, "When I stand before God at the end of my life, I would hope that I would not have a single bit of talent left, and I could say, 'I used everything you gave me.'"

"We do not remember days, we remember moments" (**Cesare Pavese**).

Celebrate today, create moments to be recalled, and live in the presence of others with meaning this day.

10

Hallelujah

"Today I choose life. Every morning when I wake up I can choose joy, happiness, negativity, pain…To feel the freedom that comes from being able to continue to make mistakes and choices—today I choose to feel life, not to deny my humanity but embrace it" (**Kevyn Aucoin**).

If we have learned anything on this journey, namely, the art of letting go, we must confront ourselves and all that held us back from being fully the person we were meant to be. The challenge was not only dealing with those issues but being able to replace them with positive steps that allowed each of us to reach goals we had not imagined possible before. Once we can do that, we are in the unique position to share with others the freedom we experience and the sense of being fully alive to all around us.

Life should be a celebration. We should not have to wait till a person dies to have a "celebration of life" in their memory. We can celebrate it if we embrace all we are and share that with others as best we can. It begins today, by celebrating that we are here, we are ready and empowered to help others.

Ralph Waldo Emerson penned, "What lies behind you and lies in front of you, pales in comparison to what lies inside of you." The essence of who you are as a woman or man has to shine forth. Whether we are single, married, divorced, separated, or belong to a religious community or commune, the person we are is to be recognized and celebrated. That will not happen if we do not allow others to see, hear, and respect us. We must have confidence in ourselves and know our self-worth and what we bring to any discussion or decision-making process.

Nor shall we fret or be bothered that we are not perfect, the storybook role model. We are not a storybook person. However, it could be argued that our life has been like a book.

How many of us simply enjoy reading? It could be magazine articles, paperback books, hardbound novels, or eBooks. If you are like me, you find that we often skim some chapters because they are boring or not written well. On the other hand, we read other chapters thoroughly, maybe even more than once. They make you think and reflect, bringing a smile, a chuckle or two, or perhaps even a frown from you. But we devour every word on the page, wondering what is coming next. Sometimes, we put the publication down, only to come back to it and read what is happening to the characters or try to solve the mystery without jumping to the last chapter before time.

Our lives are much like that to the outsider. Some parts are fascinating while others are probably routine and boring. However, in our lives, those times are worth going over repeatedly. Seeing how they shaped us, brought us to this moment, and propelled us to keep going. Those are worth keeping, sharing, and celebrating. It is not sinful pride to speak of what has worked, what you have learned over the years, and what gave you the most joy and sense of fulfillment. "Self-pride stinks," my late mother used to say. Maybe it does to some. Without it, we cower behind others, allowing them to stand out when their lives are no different from our own. Each accomplishment you have had should be recognized, acknowledged, and celebrated. Every time you were excited to see your children come home or thrilled about starting a new school year and meeting the students for the first time. Recall the day you began a new job in a new place, knowing you were hired because you had something they needed—now that you can be proud of, and it does not stink.

They are moments meant to be celebrated, talked about, and enjoyed. We share events, not worrying about being accused of prideful conceit but being true to who we are, what we experienced, and how it felt. You could call them hallelujah moments.

We were never meant to be sour-faced individuals who always see the bad or the lurking evil around every corner. Enough naysayers are walking around that you do not have to be one of them. You have a greater purpose in life.

Jennifer James told us, "If you had to choose only two qualities to get you through times of change, the first should be a sense of self-worth and the second a sense of humor." The value of self-worth has been the underlying principle of all that has been written. It allows us to share openly with others the struggles we have known and the failures we have experienced and endured. It also permits us to celebrate the moments of jubilation when we are free of all that restricted or limited who we could be.

"Owning our story and loving ourselves through that process is the bravest thing that we'll ever do" (**Brene' Brown**).

That arduous work has brought us to this point of freedom and celebration. Life is accepting the challenges of this moment. We do that because we accept that the past is history. A new chapter is being written or unfolded at this very moment. **Shannon**

L. Alder said, "When you stop living your life based on what others think of you real life begins. At that moment, you will finally see the door of self-acceptance opened." The beauty in that is knowing it is your life, your vital existence. You exist for a reason. Your life has infinite meaning because you are. What we bring about currently is up to us. We do not need to worry about what might be; we need to deal with what is. "Be happy with what you have and are, be generous with both, and you won't have to hunt for happiness" (**William E. Gladstone**).

Martha Washington wrote, "I am determined to be cheerful and happy in whatever situation I may find myself. For I have learned that the greater part of our misery or unhappiness is determined not by our circumstance but by our disposition." Allow others to see today that you are content, happy, forgiving, and most importantly, living in the moment. Freed from old baggage, but free to love and be loved.

Martin Luther King Jr. preached, "We must develop and maintain the capacity to forgive. He who is devoid of the power to forgive is devoid of the power to love. There is some good in the worst of us and some evil in the best of us. When we discover this, we are less prone to hate our enemies." In other words, we find that we can let go and be fully alive to all around us. **Deborah Day** wrote, "Lighten up on yourself. No one is perfect. Gently accept your humanness." If we are going to celebrate fully, we have to accept our own flaws and imperfections and not allow them to rule the day. We are more, as we have seen in previous chapters, than one part of our personhood. As humans, we are complex creatures. In that complexity, we will have both strong and weak points. We build on one and accept the other. We quickly learn that there are more pleasing aspects than negative aspects of us. Learn to cherish the first and not repeat the latter.

"Find the love you seek, by first finding the love within yourself. Learn to rest in that place within you that is your true home" (**Sri Ravi Shanker**).

Our celebration of life is not solitary but inclusive of everyone around us. We give, and we receive. At times, we are needy; at others, we are the shoulder to lean upon. Embrace those who need to be held and lifted up on this day. Please do not walk away or pretend not to notice them. On another day, it may well be you who needs that help or a listening ear, and they might lend it to you. **Max de Pree** said, "We need to give each other the space to grow, to be ourselves, to exercise our diversity. We need to give each other space so that we may both give and receive such beautiful things as ideas, openness, dignity, joy, healing, and inclusion."

Today, we are so consumed with work, projects, and activities that we can quickly lose sight of what is happening before us. It is elementary not to see small acts of kindness, moments of human tenderness, and generosity because we are so busy with our work that we have no time to notice. Life is full of those times, but we can be blind to the most obvious of things. As the scriptures remind us, we may have eyes to see but do not see. We must open our eyes and see what lies before us. Take the time today to inhale deeply the gentle breeze that blows across our faces as we rush from one meeting and engagement to the next. Let it relax you and refocus your vision.

Ashley Montagu stated, "The moments of happiness we enjoy take us by surprise. It is not that we seize them but that they seize us." And when they take hold of you, stop what you are doing and enjoy. Never let such moments pass you by because you were too busy to celebrate them. Meetings come and go. Endless chatter that only calls for more meetings or committee assignments. I assure you; we will never run out of committees to belong to or meetings to attend. What we do run out of is time for ourselves. It is precious time to sit and reflect on how far we have come. We need to allow ourselves a great sigh of relief from all that has happened and all that still can be.

"Did I offer peace today? Did I bring a smile to someone's face? Did I forgive? Did I love? These are the real questions. I must trust that the little bit of love that I sow now will bear many fruits, here in this world and the life to come" (**Henri Nouwen**).

Today, we can be instruments of significant change. We have transformed ourselves into better people by letting go of what hindered our growth. And for that, we must be thankful.

Listen to these words: "Gratitude helps you to grow and expand gratitude brings joy and laughter into the lives of all those around you" (**Eileen Caddy**).

11

Believers of God or Higher Power

"Life is a series of natural and spontaneous changes. Don't resist them—that only creates sorrow. Let reality be reality. Let things flow naturally forward in whatever way they like" (**Leo Tzu**).

All believers in God hold that we are only here for a while and that circumstances, geography, and identity limit our journey. If all my life I lived in the slums of Calcutta, that would be my reality. Yes, movies or TV, if we had one, would show us another world outside what has been taken as how all people live. Perhaps I was born in the mountains of Appalachia. A family of eight all living in a three-room shack with no flooring except the clay it was built on, where water is carried from the well down the road or the stream nearby, and if lucky, your lifespan might be about forty years. Where we live, what we grew up with, and how we associated with it all helped form our view of life and the world.

Yet believers knew that all things were passing. That glory we could only imagine awaited those who believed. Death became not something to be feared but just a passing on. "Are we passing on to what?" one may ask. Some say paradise, heaven, nirvana, the kingdom of God, eternal bliss—all names we give to what we do not understand. We understand that we are called to more than the time we spend on this planet. The believer knows that we shall not rot in the Earth. Our spirit, the core of who I am, will live on—maybe not as I know it now, but I will live on. The life, death, and resurrection of Jesus assure us that for those who believe life is not ended, simply changed. As we saw earlier, at birth life as we knew it in the womb change dramatically, but we were freed at that moment to be our person.

When I was in college studying for my degree in philosophy, hearing what men and women had said and written about life, death, and the after-world made me question what to believe and hold as accurate. One of my professors was from Canada and was very sharp and astute. He taught us about philosophers who believed in eternity and those who held that when death came, that was the end. Professor Arnold ensured we were exposed to male and female philosophers and the unique perspectives each brought to the argument.

One evening, I went to his study and asked if I could talk to him. He warmly invited me in and asked me to sit. Once seated, he asked what was on my mind. I told him that I was not sure there was a God. All around me, I saw people hating one another simply because of their ethnic origins. We were living through race riots, the Cuban missile crisis, and the possibility of an all-out war. I had worked that Easter vacation in some of the poorest sections of Kentucky and saw poverty as I had never experienced it back in New Jersey. If there was a God, how could some be treated so horribly while others enjoyed real luxury or at least all essentials for a living?

I studied in a state where its most significant event was the Kentucky Derby. Some of the finest horses ran in it each year, and everyone, including many of us college students, placed bets on their favorite horse to win. Now, gambling and drinking were not allowed on campus in those days.

Professor Arnold looked me straight in the eyes and said, "John, I cannot prove to you that there is a God or that one does not exist." He then stopped his train of thought and asked if I had placed a bet on a horse in the Derby. I hesitated since I knew I could be in deep trouble for gambling. He knew what I was thinking, smiled, and said, "Remember, I am the vice president of this college, and if I cannot remember what you answer when you walk out the door, what trouble could you be in?" He then told me that after spending his adult life studying philosophers before him, there was a 50-50 percent chance there was a God. So, he was placing his bet on the fact that there was and living his life accordingly. Where would I place my bet, looking at the odds? I have never forgotten those words.

Do we not read in **Psalm 30:18**, "Truly, the LORD is waiting to be gracious to you, truly, he shall rise to show mercy; For the LORD is a God of justice: happy are all who wait for him." Believers of all faiths have held onto the belief that God blesses those who keep his word in life and prepares a place for them.

Who are the blessed? In **James 5:11**, we are told, "Indeed we call blessed those who have persevered." You have heard of the perseverance of Job, and you have seen the purpose of the Lord, because "the Lord is compassionate and merciful."

Generations of believers have held onto the belief that the mercy of God is greater than any offense we may have done if we seek forgiveness and follow the way of righteousness.

"Just as treasures are uncovered from the earth, so virtue appears from good deeds, and wisdom appears from a pure and peaceful mind. To walk safely through the maze of human life, one needs the light of wisdom and the guidance of virtue" (**Buddha**).

The holy books of our different faiths all speak of the joys of eternal life for the believer. The nonbeliever mocks our willingness to endure and push on as we strive to be more perfect. The nonbelievers only have these limited days here on Earth. Naturally, they will criticize you for believing in what you cannot see. And yet, we continue to believe. We continued to endure and do not fear the moment of death. We have placed more than a bet on the fact that there is a God, a life after this; we have committed our journey to that reality.

How many people we personally know had told us as they approached their death that they could see those who went before them gathered around the room waiting for them to join them? They physically reach out, try to touch those they see, and embrace the love surrounding them. I have witnessed it all too frequently not to believe that there is life after death.

This author believes that we are all asked two essential questions as believers. The first is obvious: Did you believe in God or a power greater than your own in your lifetime? The second is: In your days on

Earth, did you try to do what was right and just in your dealings with others?

Note that we are not asked if we succeed every day in our effort to believe or do what is right and just. But did we try?

I tell you, for all who can say, YES, I did my best always to believe that there is a God and power that draws me toward it, and YES, I tried to do what was right and just in my dealings with others. We will hear God say, "Welcome into the place I have prepared for you from all eternity. The Kingdom of God is yours."

And God will embrace us as a beloved son or daughter.

Hallelujah, amen! I shout it again, hallelujah, amen!

ACKNOWLEDGMENTS

Quotations attributed to individual writers were obtained from BrainyQuotes.Com. The Academy of American Poets for "IF" by R. Kipling.

The author is indebted to readers who have contributed insight and corrections to this work. I thank Sr. Helem Malolepsy, SSM, for her perspective as a religious sister and her corrective insights, comments, and suggestions. They made this work much better to read and reflect on. The Rev. Allan Parker Post, a spiritual humanist minister, for his consul on their perspective of life and death.

Any errors in the content or format are mine alone.

Finally, I would like to acknowledge the editorial staff from Covenant Books for their expertise, suggestions, corrections, and diligent assistance in preparing this work for final publication.

APPENDIX

The author chose the artwork of NEOSiAM, in Pexels, 2024, for the cover of this book because it bespoke one of the majestic transformations in nature that take place every year. Trees, especially maple trees, turn to wonderful shades of red, orange, and gold before they drop their leaves in the fall.

During fall, nature sheds the leaves and needles of the previous year to prepare for winter and its period of dormancy. However, come spring, they will replenish all they dropped with new leaves, needles, and coverings.

For this author, the painting simply reflected the essence of this book: the necessity we all have of shedding what no longer serves us well, not fearing our dormancy, knowing that we, too, will come back stronger, fuller, and more alive once again. Nature reminds us each year that the art of letting go is perfectly alright and beneficial.

ABOUT THE AUTHOR

Rev. Dr. John G. Pisarcik has given retreats, work-shops, and seminars nationally and internationally.

Most of his active ministry was in the field of education. He has taught at all levels, from elementary to graduate schools. He served as a principal of private and regional high schools and taught ethics in a graduate school of theology. He was director of ministry programs at the university level and a faculty member of the summer faculty for doctoral candidates. He holds a bachelor's degree in philosophy, two masters degrees, and a doctorate in sacred theology/ministry.

Previously published books:

Ramblings of an Old Man
*Hard Choices for Christians: A Collection of
    Contemporary Essays*
Naughty or Nice—Virtue or Vice: Which will it be?
Death to the Bishop
My Name is James
My Name is James: The Sequel

The above can be obtained from the CreateSpacestore.com, Amazon.com, Kindle.com, Barnes and Noble, and Covenantbooks.com